THE ART OF MANIFESTING MONEY

How To Manifest Money Using The Law Of Attraction

REBECCA COLLINS

The content contained within this book may not be reproduced, duplicated or transmitted without direct written permission from the author or the publisher.

Under no circumstances will any blame or legal responsibility be held against the publisher, or author, for any damages, reparation, or monetary loss due to the information contained within this book. Either directly or indirectly. You are responsible for your own choices, actions, and results.

Disclaimer Notice:

Please note the information contained within this document is for educational and entertainment purposes only. All effort has been executed to present accurate, up to date, and reliable, complete information. No warranties of any kind are declared or implied. Readers acknowledge that the author is not engaging in the rendering of legal, financial, medical or professional advice. The content within this book has been derived from various sources. Please consult a licensed professional before attempting any techniques outlined in this book.

By reading this document, the reader agrees that under no circumstances is the author responsible for any losses, direct or indirect, which are incurred as a result of the use of the information contained within this document, including, but not limited to, — errors, omissions, or inaccuracies.

Copyright Notice

All rights reserved.

No part of this book may be reproduced in any form or by any electronic or mechanical means, including information storage and retrieval systems, without written permission from the author, except for the use of brief quotations in a book review.

Under no circumstances will any blame or legal responsibility be held against the publisher, or author, for any damages, reparation, or monetary loss due to the information contained within this book. Either directly or indirectly. You are responsible for your own choices, actions, and results.

FTC Disclosure, some links in this book may be affiliate links. This means that the Author/Publisher will receive some compensation in the form of commission from the sale of the product.

Enjoy the book.

Worldwide Copyright held at Copyright House, London EC2R 8AY, England.

Copyright Rebecca Collins 2021 - All rights reserved.

CONTENTS

Introduction — vii

1. Rich Mind vs. Poor Mind — 1
2. The Money Trap & How To Get Out Of It — 12
3. Law of Attraction Secrets — 24
4. Manifesting Money - The Ultimate Power — 37
5. How Visualization Works — 53
6. How to Connect The Dots — 66
7. Powerful Affirmations To Attract Money To you — 78
8. Bending The Universe – Taking Back Control — 92

Conclusion — 105

INTRODUCTION

Millions of people all over the world talk about how the Law of Attraction has transformed their lives for the better. Wherever you turn, you'll read rags to riches stories and we've all heard celebrities talking about how they have achieved phenomenal success by using the law.

Maybe you've tried it yourself and so far aren't convinced that it actually works, or can't understand what you have been doing wrong.

This book is about to change all that!

The law of attraction has become mainstream – everyone is talking about it but most people still don't know it's secret.

People get excited when they first discover the Law of Attraction but many miss its most crucial message. They assume it's all about having happy thoughts and waiting for magic to happen overnight. Others try it for a while and give up far too soon because they don't see immediate results.

This is NOT the way to use the Law of Attraction and I'm going to tell you why.

If you are new to the subject, you may be wondering what all the fuss is about and are curious to find out more. I'm here to reveal its deepest secrets and give you the help you need to leverage the law to its full advantage.

What exactly is the Law of Attraction?

It is ancient wisdom that has always existed, based on the belief that:

- Our thoughts are energy that the universe responds to.
- Positive thinking brings positive outcomes.
- Negative thinking brings negative outcomes.
- We can manifest wealth, happiness and success, simply by thinking them into being.

In other words, if you think positively, you will attract positive outcomes in all aspects of your life, including health, relationships, and your finances. The same applies to negative thoughts, which bring negative results. Basically, what goes around comes around.

The law states that like attracts like, so the more positive you are about life, the more abundance you will enjoy. By removing negativity from your way of thinking, you also create more space for good things to happen.

You can ALWAYS improve your circumstances if you are open to the possibility and get rid of negative self-talk. And the more good vibes you give out, the more you will receive in return.

The master of Taoism, Lao Tzu, described it beautifully when he said that our thoughts become words, which then become actions, then habits, forming our character and finally our destiny.

We can only utilize the Law of Attraction to our advantage when we fully understand how it works.

It isn't an instant money-making scheme or a get-rich-quick hustle and there's no quick way to get what you want in life. The law does exist, but if you don't use it correctly, it's not going to work for you.

I am aware that many people think that the law of attraction is some kind of pseudoscience, claiming that there's no concrete evidence to prove that it works. That simply isn't the case, and there is a wealth of scientific research to debunk that idea.

I've attended many seminars and workshops on cognitive psychology, which explains our mental processes, and have applied a lot of that knowledge in my work. Positive thinking is definitely one of the techniques I use to empower others to achieve their goals and the law of attraction fits right in with that approach.

You will learn in this book how to manifest your desires by following some specific strategies.

Neuroscientists are starting to understand how repeated habits and thoughts can rewire our brains and provide even greater possibilities for us to succeed. Just by practicing visualization, for example, our brain starts emitting certain hormones that get us into success mode.

Psychologists use the power of positive thinking all the time in their work and a lot of counselling techniques apply methods very similar to the law of attraction. It's even been proven that you have more chance of succeeding if you are optimistic and focus all of your energy on doing just that.

Did you know that you create your reality through what you think and feel, whether you are conscious of it or not?

When you learn how to harness the power of your thoughts, you can direct them in ways that will bring you abundance. Feelings like enthusiasm, joy, and appreciation are full of positive energy and if you send them out, you will attract people and opportunities that resonate on the same positive wavelength.

On the other hand, feeling pessimistic, negative, and angry will only attract the same negative people and events into your life.

Who wouldn't love to have all of their dreams fulfilled?

If you are talking about happiness, most of us wish that we had more money. We all know that money in itself can't buy happiness, but it sure goes a long way to improving our quality of life. It makes us feel more secure and allows us to do the things we enjoy, instead of being restricted by lack of funds.

One of the main reasons why we find it so difficult to make more money is because we limit our potential. We get stuck in badly paid jobs, feel powerless to break free of our daily grind, don't tap into our creative side, bury our ambitions, and prefer to moan about the problem instead of doing anything about it.

Not having money or enough of it hangs over us like a dead weight, making us feel miserable, depressed, and hopeless. The idea that we can actually use our thoughts and energy to manifest money seems impossible because if it was so easy, wouldn't everybody be doing it? Well, the reason they don't is because they have a negative relationship with money in the first place.

Most people think they will never be wealthy or ever have a continuous supply of money to sustain them. It's understandable when you consider that we have to work hard to earn a salary and many of us struggle to balance our ingoings with our outgoings.

Debt, financial worry, and the inability to handle our expenses efficiently mean we're always chasing after the next dollar. It's exhausting and most folk can't see the wood for the trees. They are so involved in trying to make money through hard slog that they don't realize they are sabotaging their chances of success while doing so.

The law of attraction says that negative energy attracts negative energy. For example, if you believe you will never be rich then, the chances are that you won't because you've already accepted that as a fact.

You get what you wish for, good or bad. If instead, you positively affirm that good things will come, and manifest that idea in your mind, you will be able to achieve your dreams.

Positive thinking isn't enough.

You need to do other things such as sticking to your goals and being aligned with your intentions. It's no different from wanting to lose weight: you have to follow a calorie-controlled diet and an exercise regime to do that. But if you also visualize a slimmer, healthier self and use positive affirmations in your life, you are much more likely to get to your desired weight.

Those of you who have tried to shed pounds in the past will know that it's not enough to be disciplined – if you don't put all of your positivity into it, you will give up very easily at the first opportunity.

Once you learn the art of manifesting money, you'll realize it's not like you will wake up tomorrow and find piles of dollar bills in your living room, or that your bank balance has magically jumped to a six-figure number. That would be impossible, right?

What manifesting more money means is applying certain thought patterns and behaviors that will eventually bring you what you are seeking.

It all comes down to the fact that the Universe responds to the positive energy you put out there and rewards you with positive results, while negative energy brings only negative results.

What I can say for sure is that you have nothing to lose. So many people have benefitted from the law of attraction that it's worth giving it a shot. I believe that anything is possible if we focus on our goals and work towards them with the conviction that we will succeed. A little help from the Universe can make all the difference, so why not start applying this idea in your life as of today?

I'm going to be walking you through the different ways you can do that in the following chapters. I'll also explain how your thoughts are powerful sources of energy that you can use to attract abundance into your life, particularly money. The truth is that most of us are fixated on making more, but are going about it the completely wrong way.

In this book, you will learn how to invest your energy the right way so that you can unlock your potential through a range of practical exercises and tips, such as:

The power of having a rich mindset: how to stop thinking 'poor' and start getting 'rich'.

Ways to get out of the money trap: escaping the poverty trap by forming new neural pathways.

The real secrets of the law of attraction: the tried and tested science behind the myth.

How to manifest money: creating new strategies that will eliminate money blocks.

The benefits of visualization: the power of your imagination has no limits.

The strength of affirmations: using your words to stop self-sabotaging your dreams.

How to bend the Universe: tuning in to what the Universe is telling you and how to make things happen.

If you don't believe in your ability to transform your life for the better, then your life isn't going to change. It will remain exactly the same and you'll continue to wish for things you will never attain.

But if you nurture a strong belief in your abilities to create change, you will learn how to get into the mindset of striving for them and have much more chance of success. As the old saying goes, you can do anything when you put your mind to it.

Are you ready to manifest your dreams of making more money?

If so, let's GO and discover how to do just that!

1

RICH MIND VS. POOR MIND

"Many folks think they aren't good at earning money when what they don't know is how to use it." – Frank A. Clark

Some people seem to have a knack for accumulating more and more money, while others are constantly complaining about the lack of it. My friend Elaine, for instance, is one of the wealthiest women in the UK, although you wouldn't know it to look at her.

She still lives in the old cottage she bought in 1995 for 80,000 pounds, her normal attire is jeans and a T-shirt, and her everyday mode of transport is a bike. But, she has a large steady income, is always open to new investment opportunities, and leads a happy, healthy life.

On the other hand, my old school chum Tod is forever in debt, can't seem to hold down a job for more than a few months, and has just bought himself a new Range Rover. His attitude to money is to spend it even when he doesn't have it and this bad habit means that he is often completely broke.

When I think about the two people I mentioned above, it's obvious to me that each of them has a very different relationship with money. In fact, they both have a totally different mindset, which affects their attitude to making money in the first place.

It's not that Elaine is more clever than Tod. She wasn't born into money or had it handed down to her on a silver platter. Tod isn't lacking in skills or potential and comes from quite a wealthy background. They both just view money and the making of it in completely opposite ways, with the result that one of them is successful while the other isn't.

This is very typical of the population as a whole. While some of us seem to attract wealth, others of us attract a lack of it.

Everyone would love to live an abundant life, where money is no problem and we have a regular stream of it trickling into our bank account, but many people just can't seem to manage that. They even have trouble imagining that they could ever be in a better financial position and believe they will never achieve success.

This is clearly a mindset problem and is directly related to the law of attraction, which states that negative thoughts bring negative consequences.

If you don't have the right approach to acquiring wealth in your life, then it will always escape you. Even winning the Lottery is extremely unlikely. The reason is that you have closed off your mind to the possibility that you will ever be prosperous. The way to get around that is by adopting a 'rich' mindset, instead of a 'poor' one.

How exactly do you do that?

Well, let's take a look at where you could be going wrong first of all, before going over the strategies to help turn things around.

What's your money mindset?

All of us have preconceived notions about life, which shape our way of thinking. We are influenced by a number of factors such as upbringing, family, personal experiences, peer groups, education, and culture. Some of us are brought up thinking that success is within our grasp, while others are taught that only the 'lucky' ones ever achieve anything.

But no matter what your own story is, this doesn't mean that you are tied to it and can't bring about changes in your life. To do that, you need to revise your mindset – your way of looking at the world in relation to your dreams.

You can begin by taking a look at the statements below and ticking the ones that most closely match your relationship with money. Feel free to choose more than one if they apply to you:

1. I believe that money makes money
2. I see money as something to be earned
3. I live according to my needs and not my desires
4. I always overspend
5. I don't care about trends, only about net worth
6. I care about new trends and my image
7. I invest a proportion of my income
8. I work paycheque to paycheque
9. I work because I enjoy it
10. I work because I have to
11. I set long-term money goals
12. I don't have any savings
13. I am prepared to take calculated investment risks
14. I avoid taking financial risks

15. I'm not afraid to take advice from others
16. I don't enjoy seeking advice from others
17. I believe everyone can make money
18. I believe you are either born rich or not
19. I make sure I always have money put aside
20. I am usually in debt

Which of the above did you tick? Here's the thing: if you ticked more *even* than *odd* numbers, (i.e. you ticked 2, 4, 6, 8, 10, and so on) you probably have a poor relationship with money.

Unlike those who ticked more odd numbers (1, 3, 5, etc.), you are not making money because your attitude is all wrong.

In essence, you are setting yourself up for failure and need to completely rethink your whole strategy if you want to improve your chances of securing a steady source of income.

If you come from a background where social issues are contributing to a life of poverty, you may feel that there's no way out of that. It could be that you see rich people as being inherently different from you, or that they are lucky, privileged, or greedy.

In reality, it's not about rich people versus poor people. They aren't your enemy and there are plenty of wealthy people who started off with a similar background to your own.

At the same time, I can think of lots of people born into money who squandered it very quickly. What makes everyone different is the mindset they have, which is the crux of success or failure in financial terms.

What is a 'rich' mindset?

Everyone would like to have more money and live a life of abundance. Unfortunately, if you believe that you will never be able to achieve that, you will be unable to apply the law of attraction, which states that your mind can manifest whatever it desires.

Denying that possibility from the outset means you aren't even giving yourself a chance. On the other hand, someone who cultivates a 'rich' mindset, knows that the law of attraction works and they leverage it to the full.

How can you do the same?

Forget the idea that most people with money live in enormous mansions, drive Ferraris, and flash their money off at every opportunity.

Some do, but most of those with a 'rich' mentality aren't interested in luxury items, fast cars, or superyachts. The vast majority are ordinary people who have built up their assets over the years and don't always feel the need to flaunt what they have. Having a 'rich' mentality is more about securing money than spending it.

A 'rich' mindset involves breaking free of the cycle of poverty you may find yourself in. Sitting and wishing it will change is fine, but it's not enough. In order for the law of attraction to work, you have to BELIEVE that you can turn things around, and be prepared to apply that optimism in all aspects of your life.

You can start by changing your view that your circumstances are fixed and will never change. If you are in a low-paid job that merely serves to cover your basic expenses like rent, utility bills, and groceries, you need to readjust your goals. Nothing will change if YOU aren't prepared to change.

A 'rich' mindset sees challenges as something to overcome and accepts that life is never easy. Everyone goes through difficult times and even the most successful people have to deal with rough patches in their lives. But that doesn't stop them from moving ahead in pursuit of their goals.

I can think of many well-known personalities who had difficult beginnings in life, but who went on to achieve wealth and success. People like Oprah Winfrey, Starbucks chairman and CEO Howard Schultz, the designer Ralph Lauren, writer J.K. Rowling, to name but a few. None of these well-known names were born with money, but all persisted in their vision for a better life. If they can do it, so can you!

Rich people always have a vision. They have set themselves goals and are prepared to work towards them. They don't expect instant success or rely on luck, but focus on the end result and are prepared to put the time and effort into making their vision become a reality.

When you are full of hopes and dreams for your future, everything is possible but if you feel disheartened and uninspired, how can you expect anything to come to fruition?

Those with a 'rich' mindset don't waste their time unproductively. Instead, they have established routines that are intentionally created to make the most of life. That doesn't include scrolling through their social media all day or bingeing on their favorite streaming channel.

What it does mean is their daily routine includes being with the right people and putting themselves in an environment that encourages growth, not stagnation. How you manage your time is also important and discipline is a key factor. Instead of wasting the day away, the 'rich' mindset involves working when you need to, in a place that will help you to be productive without distractions.

If you can manage to stick to a routine where you stay focused for a few hours each day and keep company with like-minded people, you are on the way to success.

Having a 'rich' mindset means being results-driven.
When you have set your goals, every action you take after that should be aligned with achieving the best outcome. Your whole day will be geared towards getting results – maybe not instantaneously – but in the foreseeable future.

Often, we wish for something in general, such as having more money, without narrowing it down to an exact goal. Instead of having vague ambitions, you should commit to a specific target, for example, "I will set up my business by the end of the year", or, "I will earn 10,000 dollars in six months." This makes it a lot easier to really go for it!

When someone with a 'rich' mindset doesn't know the answer, they are prepared to ask. The most successful entrepreneurs are those who had the common sense and humility to ask for advice. No one knows it all and wealthy people are the first to admit that. They seek to expand their knowledge in a particular subject, are prepared to up-skill, and ask smart questions.

This is because they are in tune with their goals and understand the challenges ahead, which leads to greater success in the long run. They don't brag that they know everything or dismiss ideas without really listening first and are more open to new opportunities than you would probably believe.

People with a 'rich' mindset don't work for money. Contrary to what you may think, it's not about chasing the dollar for them but is more about growth and contribution, knowing that this is the best way to achieve their goals.

Working just for the sake of increasing your bank balance isn't necessarily bad, but if you don't invest your time and energy in growth, you probably won't experience any.

Someone with a 'rich' mindset surrounds themselves with like-minded people. They understand the value of inspiring acquaintances and are willing to learn from them. They may also seek counsel from a mentor or coach, who can give them the tools to make a success of their lives.

Equally, part of having a 'rich' mindset is giving to others, sharing your wisdom, and helping those around you to succeed. The more good you do for others, the more good will come your way.

When you have a 'rich' mindset, you are always on the lookout for new opportunities. Investors are visionaries who can see the potential in the market and will be ready to put time and money into anything that they feel will reap returns. They usually see outside of the box and know that even when the economy is at a low, opportunities are always out there.

It's during times of economic hardship that the 'rich' mindset differentiates itself from the 'poor' one and you only have to think about the old saying, 'One man's trash is another man's treasure' to realize that this is so true.

Those with a 'rich' mindset learn how to manage their money. None of us are born as financial experts and we all need to learn the skills of handling money. Some people are very good at it and others, not so much. I always felt I was useless at managing my finances and it wasn't until I found a good accountant that I learned how to handle my income better.

Instead of spending it willy nilly, I realized the importance of making a budget and sticking to it. This is a priority for anyone who wants to achieve financial growth without getting into debt.

You aren't afraid to fail when you have a 'rich' mindset. On the contrary, you see failure as a lesson to be learned and a stepping stone to success. Once difficulties arise, these people look for solutions and don't get stressed out or lose hope.

They persevere, seeing each hurdle as being one step nearer to their goals, and view failure as a valuable life lesson. They learn not to make the same mistakes again and seek out different approaches to get to the finish line, as any true winner would do.

Lastly, and perhaps most importantly, someone with a 'rich' mindset believes firmly in abundance. They don't adhere to the belief that resources are limited, that opportunities are few and far between, or that other people's success means less chance of them succeeding.

They embrace the idea that life is full of possibilities for all and will welcome the success of their peers, rather than feeling resentful or jealous. Their positivity shines through everything they do and they are convinced they can achieve their goals. A person with a 'poor' mindset differs greatly from someone with a 'rich' mindset. They believe that they will have achieved everything they have ever dreamed of at a specific point in the future.

They think that the goal is to retire and to sit around relaxing for the rest of their life, living off any pension payments or savings that they may have. This is the total opposite of a growth mindset, which sets no limits to the abundance of opportunities in life. If you dislike your work so much that you want to retire, think about all of the other exciting activities you could pursue that may generate extra income after that.

Many people realize very late in life that they can still make money after retirement, but in a completely different context. Instead of waiting around for their monthly payment, they are actively seeking out new opportunities and investing in the rest of their future.

But you don't have to wait until you retire to start enjoying life. You can begin today and with hard work, consistency, and positivity, create wealth in the here and now. You can start by asking yourself three important questions and then apply the law of attraction to fulfill your dreams.

A: *What is your vision?*

B: *Where are you going?*

C: *What kind of life do you want?*

Spend some time to write down what is driving you and where you want to go. Make a long-term vision that is divided up into smaller milestones and always keep the full picture in your mind. Remind yourself every day of your vision and continue to keep it in sight despite any obstacles you meet on the way.

Try not to focus on how rich you want to be, but how having more money can improve your life and make you a better person.

This is a good way to begin applying the law of attraction in your life, even if you feel trapped by your present circumstances. You may live well below the minimum wage/salary or find it hard to make ends meet. The situation can seem so hopeless that you don't believe you can ever rise above it.

In the next chapter, I am going to explain how you can overcome this mental block and help you to use the law of attraction to get out of the poverty trap. As long as you believe it is possible, you can achieve it!

Key Points:

- *Having the right mindset is the secret to acquiring wealth in your life.*
- *It's better to secure money than to spend it.*
- *You need to believe that you can change your life.*
- *Life is never going to be a walk in the park and you will always face problems.*
- *Having a vision is the most important plan you can make.*
- *Use your time and energy productively.*
- *Be prepared to ask when you don't know the answers.*
- *Stay focused on your goals and be open to new opportunities.*
- *Learn about managing money and seek guidance or advice.*
- *Surround yourself with inspiring people.*
- *Trust in the abundance of the universe.*

2

THE MONEY TRAP & HOW TO GET OUT OF IT

"You are the master of your destiny. You can influence, direct and control your own environment. You can make your life what you want it to be." – Napoleon Hill

Poverty isn't just an economic predicament created by political, social, or cultural dynamics. It's also a psychological mindset that can feel like being in an actual prison.

If you have ever been in the poverty trap, as it is often called, or are currently struggling to make ends meet, I understand exactly how you feel. I myself grew up in a large family and money was often tight. With so many mouths to feed, we had to make do with very little and my parents were always stressed about how to pay the next bills or buy essential items. That sense of hopelessness and inability to see any light at the end of the tunnel can be truly disheartening.

It's a well-known fact that the poverty trap is a real social problem affecting millions of people all over the world. There are many reasons why this is the case and it usually comes down to external factors, although not always. There are many unforeseen situations that can bring about poverty.

An illness, accident, or addiction for example can contribute to anyone becoming impoverished, while losing one's main source of income is another common problem. You may have inherited generational poverty from your family, which creates psychological and behavioral barriers to achieving prosperity.

Lack of education and peer pressure might also prevent someone from striving to fulfill their potential and being surrounded by others with a poverty mindset can 'normalize' it to a certain extent.

I do want to make a distinction here between the poverty trap as a social phenomenon and having a 'poverty mindset'. Although the two often have very different root causes, I believe that both can be alleviated by applying the law of attraction.

It may seem impossible to get out of the poverty trap if you live in a society where there is a widespread lack of resources or no political will to improve living conditions. This book isn't about trying to fix the world's problems (which is a very big topic), so I want to focus on you as an individual and help you to overcome whatever personal constraints are holding you back.

By understanding the law of attraction and adopting some life-changing strategies, there is hope, no matter what your circumstances are.

What is a poverty mindset?

It depends on who you talk to because each of us has a unique perspective on our circumstances. You may consider yourself to be living in poverty if you have been unemployed for a long period of time, or you might feel that you are stuck in an economic rut even though you work and receive a basic salary. What's interesting here isn't so much the situation you find yourself in, but how you view it. This is the poverty mindset, which affects every aspect of your life and prevents you from attracting wealth.

Funnily enough, the more you believe that you are stuck on this economic hamster wheel, the more difficult it is for you to get off it.

This is where the law of attraction really comes into its own, by helping you to get rid of that mindset of hopelessness, misery, and resignation. You can change your life, as long as you really want to.

Often, we cling to a particular way of seeing the world because we haven't realized there is any other alternative. The law of attraction invites you to have an open mind and to think positively, even when everything around you seems like doom and gloom.

You may not even be aware that your mindset is stopping you from fulfilling your dreams, but if you can relate to any of the following, then you will realize that your poverty mindset might be holding you back.

Lack of ambition

Do you have self-limiting expectations of what you can and can't achieve? Often, those with a poverty mindset are unable to create abundance in their lives for exactly this reason. They don't set their sights high enough or take any action to bring about their dreams.

Perhaps you have been told that you will never amount to anything, or your past mistakes have left you feeling disillusioned.

Whatever image you have of yourself, know that you can change that and go on to achieve abundance in your life. Instead of settling for this sense of hopelessness, redefine who you are and release your full potential to attract more positivity than you ever thought possible.

You feel sorry for yourself

Everyone goes through hard times and it's not always easy to cope. You may have suffered an illness or trauma, perhaps you have accrued substantial personal debt, failed an important exam, lost your job, or experienced the breakdown of a relationship. All of these events can make you feel anger, sadness, grief, and frustration, which can easily lead to a sense of self-pity or a victim mentality.

That seems reasonable under the circumstances, but holding on to such negative emotions for too long can seriously damage your personal growth and chances of happiness.

Instead of asking, "Why me?" which only leaves you feeling helpless and disempowered, change the narrative. Rather than inviting more negativity into your life, start saying this powerful phrase: "It's in my hands to turn things around."

You are in control of your life and will experience more positive energy all around you when you begin to believe that.

You constantly compare yourself with others

When you compare yourself with others, this can lead to very negative feelings of envy, resentment, and bitterness. Wanting what other people have or being jealous of their accomplishments takes up a lot of energy that could be better used to get what you want. You are also denying the fact that you have your own strengths and qualities, putting yourself down in relation to others.

If you must compare yourself to someone, choose inspirational figures, learn how they have achieved success, and try to adopt some of their techniques. The one thing you will discover is that all of them maintain a positive mindset and work towards manifesting their goals and ambitions, instead of worrying about what other people are doing.

You act from a state of fear

When you have a poverty mindset, you are more focussed on avoiding the bad things that may happen to you and concentrate less on pursuing anything positive in your life.

If you face economic difficulties, it's natural for the mind to go into stress mode as you try to avoid more problems. Your brain releases the stress hormone cortisol, which increases your anxiety levels and blocks you from functioning in a productive way or allowing you to be optimistic.

Fear is a disabling emotion and an easy cycle to get into but you can prevent it from taking control. For every negative incident, look for a positive and focus on ways of improving your life instead of surrendering to fear.

You dwell on what is missing in your life

If your thoughts are dominated by statements like, "I'm sick of having no money, I don't have any prospects of getting a decent job, if only my house wasn't so small...," you are not helping yourself at all.

Obsessing over the lack of anything good in your life only feeds into your poverty mentality and offers no solution.

According to the law of attraction, if you channel all of your energy into concentrating on what you lack, you are attracting even more of a 'lack' in your life. Think of it this way: if you try to fill an empty glass with yet more air, it still remains empty. To quench your thirst and sustain your well-being, you need to keep topping the glass up with water. Drink from the fountain of abundance that is out there waiting for you instead of complaining about being in a desert.

You have a toxic relationship with money

Ok, you may be wondering what I mean by this so let me give you some examples. You believe that your lack of money is the main cause of all your problems (believe me, it isn't). You don't like spending it when you have it, skimp on buying non-essentials for fear of wasting it, and prefer to buy on the cheap.

Instead of enjoying what you have, you deny yourself even small comforts and hate having to put your hand in your pocket. You don't like treating others and will jump at any freebies if it means not having to pay.

You don't understand the value of investing money and constantly worry that you'll never have enough or that it will run out.

That's not a healthy relationship to have and it's pretty toxic if you think about it. When it comes to manifesting positive outcomes in your life, you should be thinking of all the good that money can bring rather than dwelling on its negative impact.

I'll be giving you lots of useful strategies for manifesting money later on in the book. Before that, let's discover how to break free from the confines of the poverty trap and align yourself to acquiring wealth using the law of attraction in **5 easy steps**.

Remember, nothing can be achieved without the desire to change your preconceptions. You will need to literally release yourself from any thoughts that have been holding you back so get ready to do so. It's time to start afresh and manifest your dreams.

1. See wealth in a new way

It's possible that the word 'wealth' is a loaded term for you. It can evoke a lot of negative feelings because of your lack of it. You might also associate other words like 'rich', 'prosperous', or 'loaded' with your apparent inability to ever be in that position. You need to revise these ideas and can start by seeing money not from the viewpoint of someone who doesn't have any but from one that welcomes and expects to receive it.

I'll be talking about visualization exercises in Chapter 5, but for now, just imagine for a second how it would feel to have a lot of money in your hand at this moment. I'm sure you would feel excited, less stressed, and be breathing a sigh of relief, right? Hold on to that feeling – it will do you the world of good.

You know that if you had more money, you would be able to enjoy so many things, so think of wealth as something that brings opportunity and well-being for you and your family. Once you begin to do so, you will see how you can start to attract more of it into your life.

2. Start positive self-talk

I grew up constantly hearing phrases like, "We can't afford that, it's too expensive, it's not for people like us, money doesn't grow on trees," all of which made me believe that I didn't deserve to be wealthy. I continued to tell myself this for a long time, and even developed a kind of imposter syndrome when I did start to make money. I felt like I didn't really deserve it and told myself I was just lucky.

This incessant negative self-talk can really restrict us from attracting wealth because we tell ourselves we aren't good enough or worthy of receiving it. We are actually letting a few words control our whole lives, being dictated to by a little voice in our heads that tells us it's just not our destiny to be wealthy.

This can be reversed so easily and if you have read my book entitled **Love Yourself Deeply**, you will know just how powerful self-talk can be and what to do to overcome it.

Remember that negative thoughts attract negative outcomes, so the sooner you get rid of them, the better.

3. Assume responsibility for your actions

Many people caught in the poverty trap feel totally helpless and cannot see any way out of their situation. It's as if someone has tied their hands behind their back, making it impossible for them to help themselves.

Although this obviously isn't true, it's easy to get into the habit of thinking, "There's nothing I can do... it's out of my hands...." To escape from that sense of despair, you need to realize that you alone are responsible for your thoughts and actions.

No matter how difficult things may seem, no one is forcing you to give up control of your life. You have a choice: you can continue to blame others for your lack of money or you can recognize your mistakes, learn from them, and live life your way.

Only you are accountable for whatever future lies ahead, so don't waste time letting others decide that for you.

4. Make a plan

Instead of dwelling on your misfortune and thinking about your past failures or mistakes, create a plan that will enable you to achieve your future goals. How can you go about making more money? You need to spend some time thinking about this, and then make a list of practical steps you can take.

As soon as you do so, you have already started to break free from the poverty mindset because you are taking back control of your life. Set yourself a distinct goal, such as the examples below:

- get a job
- study at college or university
- earn x amount of money in 12 months
- save a proportion of your income each month
- pay off your credit card debts by next year
- upskill to improve your chances of promotion
- double or triple your income over the next 3 years
- move to a bigger house
- take your family on vacation

Once you have set your goals, you will instantaneously feel more motivated and can work towards achieving them. If your goal is to get a job, for example, write down any steps you will need to take to make it happen. Your list could look something like this:

Week 1

- Make a resume/CV
- Print out copies
- Distribute to local businesses in person or send via email
- Don't have internet? Ask a friend for help

Week 2

- Check out current vacancies on job boards such as LinkedIn or Indeed
- Follow up on any jobs applied for
- Ask around about job openings

Week 3

- Cast your net wider than your local area
- Do some volunteer work
- Check out internships

Week 4

- Keep looking for work
- Consider all available options, even if it doesn't seem like your dream job at first
- Stay focused on how a job can change your life
- Believe that you will find something

Whatever your goal is, outline the steps you need to take to get you there.

5. Never give up

One thing that financially successful people do is persevere. They don't give up at the first hurdle and are consistent in their efforts to succeed.

It's a lot easier to call it a day at the first sign of failure, but why would you do that to yourself? If you don't succeed in the beginning, keep trying – nobody said it was going to be easy.

Do you recall the great 2006 movie with Will Smith called 'The Pursuit of Happyness?' If you haven't seen it, it's about the real-life story of Chris Gardner, a homeless salesman who struggled for over a year to find employment while taking care of his five-year-old son. Despite all of the challenges he faced, the main character never gave up.

He was relentless in his efforts to find work and focused on doing the best he could for himself and his son. After months of living on the streets and having no money at all, he finally managed to achieve his goal.

Everyone deserves a happy ending, and the only way to get there is by persevering and having the belief that you will eventually succeed. Trust that the universe will reward you for your efforts, even when you feel disheartened because the more positive you are, the stronger the vibrations you are putting out there.

It isn't easy to magically change the way you think overnight so be patient. You have probably developed a habit of limiting yourself, and negative thoughts have been dominating your inner dialogue for a long time. You may not be able to change the social system, the political situation, or the economy but believe me, you can change how you view your life.

In reality, it's not our living conditions that define us, but our own thoughts. Thinking positively can make all the difference and it has been proven time and time again the world over. From barefoot street kids who became acclaimed international sportsmen like Pele and Usain Bolt to the rags-to-riches stories of millionaires such as Shahid Khan and Dolly Parton, the world is open to you if you open up to the power of positive thinking.

So far, we've looked at how important having a positive mindset is and I've mentioned some strategies to help you escape from the poverty mentality. In the next chapter, I want to explore the law of attraction with you in more detail and reveal some of its secrets.

You will be surprised to read that you already have the power to change your life and just need to learn how to tap into that incredible energy. When you can effectively do that, your whole future becomes yours to create!

Key Points:

- *A poverty mindset will hold you back from achieving your goals.*
- *Thinking 'poor' will keep you poor.*
- *Instead of being a victim, take control of your life.*
- *Your negative emotions bring negative outcomes.*
- *Stop dwelling on what you don't have and visualize what you want.*
- *Improve your relationship with money.*
- *Follow the 5 easy steps to get out of the poverty trap.*

3

LAW OF ATTRACTION SECRETS

"What you think you become. What you feel you attract. What you imagine you create." – Buddha

Have you ever had one of those days when everything goes wrong from the moment you wake up?

You know the feeling: your alarm doesn't go off, you slip on the bathroom rug, your button comes off your shirt as you are getting dressed, you spill your coffee, your car won't start, you get to work late, you have no internet, you realize you have left your wallet at home, and so on... By the time you get home at the end of the day, you are agitated, stressed out, and totally exhausted.

These negative sequences of events seem to be unavoidable and we often put them down to Murphy's Law – the idea that 'if anything can go wrong, it will.' It's a kind of commonly held belief that we have no power to control what will happen and that bad things will occur, whether we like it or not.

But what if our expectations that negative things will happen are caused by the way we direct our energy towards that? It's not that we want to have a bad day, but by accepting that everything is going to go wrong, we are putting out negative vibes and they bounce back to us with negative outcomes.

In the same way, there may be days when you feel like you are on a roll, as if everything is working out in your favor. You wake up feeling energized, learn you have won first prize in a competition you entered, receive an email announcing you've been offered a new job, get asked out on a date, learn you have a tax refund.... How do you explain that? Coincidence? Luck?

Many people claim that this is the Law of Attraction at work, which is based on the idea that we attract what we give out – negative energy brings negative results and positive energy brings positive ones.

The law became widely known after the 2006 movie 'The Secret' was released, followed by a best-selling book of the same name. It's an ancient concept based on universal laws that have been used by many people throughout history who assert that life is what we make it. We have the ability to influence our future and manifest whatever it is we have imagined in our mind's eye.

Rather than having no control over our lives, the law of attraction states that we have absolute control if we can only learn how to think differently.

The secret is this: When we project positive energy and are optimistic about our day, there's a much greater chance that things are going to go our way. If, on the other hand, we assume the worst, that's exactly what we'll get.

It sounds pretty simple, but does it really work and if so, how can you use it to manifest your innermost desires?

I want to delve more deeply into the different principles or rules of the law so that you get a better understanding of how it can work for you. Then, we'll explore the different ways you can apply it to realize your dreams, including how to make more money.

Rule 1: Like attracts like

This means that similar things are attracted to each other, including our thoughts. If you are stuck in a negative mindset, your experiences are probably going to be negative. When you are always imagining the worst-case scenario, the chances are that this is exactly what will happen.

It's not that you are responsible for causing the bad outcomes, but you are attracting them to you with your negative thought patterns. On the other hand, if you have a positive mindset, you will receive positive experiences.

Rule 2: Nature abhors a vacuum

We can explain this by saying that if you remove negativity from your life, you are creating more space for good things to take their place. Your mind is always working, even when you are asleep, and negative thoughts are continuously reinforced.

When you get out of that negative cycle, the brain still needs something to work on, and positive thinking will fill that space. The more positively you think, the more your life will be filled with good things.

Rule 3: The present is always perfect

This is a basic premise of the law, which states that you can always do things to improve your present situation. It is actually saying that you are in control – not fate, luck, or coincidence. Even if you find yourself in a bad place at the moment, you should focus your energy on finding ways to make the best of your situation.

If you are feeling down and sorry for yourself, all of those negative vibes you are sending out will only attract more negativity. Instead, think of all the good things in your life and you will receive more of them. You have the power to make the most of your present once you open up to the possibility.

Your mindset influences everything that happens in your life so you have to be prepared to change it. Instead of being closed-minded about any prospects of obtaining happiness, you need to get rid of that defeatist, negative self-talk and believe in the power of the Universe instead. There are several ways to apply the law of attraction in your life and we are going to take a look at those in greater detail in later chapters. For now, suffice to say that they include things like:

- practicing gratitude
- visualizing your goals
- using positive affirmations
- looking for the positives
- identifying negative thinking
- reframing negatives into positives

What the Law of Attraction can and can't do

I want to make it clear that the law of attraction may not be an immediate solution to all of your problems, but it can help you to cultivate a more positive outlook and motivate you to achieve your goals.

- It **can** help you to deal with problems more effectively.
- It can't bring immediate results if you are still in a negative mind loop.
- It **can** provide the motivation you need to reach any desired outcome.

- It can't magically change your life if you aren't prepared to take action.
- It **can** be used to manifest wealth, happiness, and a more fulfilling life.
- It can't prevent external events out of your control from happening.
- It **can** give you the tools to deal with them in a positive way.

The power of positive thinking

Our world is created by thoughts. Whatever exists was once a thought in someone's mind, from the chair you are sitting on to the music you listen to. When our thoughts become actions, we can create tangible objects and experiences that shape everything around us. The same power of creativity can be used to make your dreams a reality, and it's the law of attraction that works to help you achieve that.

Everyone has heard of the benefits of positive thinking, although not all are convinced of its effectiveness. Yet, highly respected institutions like the Mayo Clinic fully support the power of positive thinking, taking into consideration years of research by qualified scientists, researchers, and medical practitioners. There is, therefore, no doubt that the way we think can improve our health, wellness, and quality of life.

The benefits of positive thinking are now widely accepted and include things like:

- Lower rates of depression
- Lower levels of stress
- Greater resistance to the common cold
- Better psychological and physical well-being
- Better cardiovascular health and reduced risk of death from cardiovascular disease

- Better coping skills during hardships and times of stress
- Increased life span

Apart from being better able to cope with stressful situations, if you are an optimist, you probably also follow a healthier lifestyle and enjoy more physical activity than a pessimist does. There's no magic to this and it's not something unattainable either.

Everyone can benefit from the power of positive thinking if they really want to. Some people seem to be optimistic by nature, while others find it hard to be positive all the time. If you are one of them, imagine how much better life can be just by changing the way you think!

How to think more positively

If you allow negative thoughts to get the better of you, you are probably a pessimist. If, on the other hand, you think mostly positive thoughts, you are more likely to be an optimist.

Positive thinking begins when you start to engage in positive self-talk. If you find that hard to do, I am certain that you realize your negative inner dialogue isn't helping you. It's not that you want to be negative by necessity, and a lot of it probably comes from past experiences or negative biases about certain situations. If, let's say, you have failed your driving test three times already, you probably believe that you are going to fail it for the fourth time. This pessimistic expectation will most likely cause you to fail because you have already told yourself you aren't going to pass and won't put the right energy into improving your skills.

Negative thinking is a bad habit that many people have gotten used to. You can learn to start thinking positively and with time, you will enjoy all the abundance that the Universe is waiting to bring you. Here are three main areas to focus on if you want to change:

Identify your negative thoughts. Consider all the things in your life that you have negative thoughts about. It could be your appearance, your job, your lack of money, your home, or your relationships. Choose one that you can begin to think of in a more positive light. For example, if you hate your job, accept you are lucky to have one at all and be thankful for it. Next, start looking for a new one or reconsider if you want a complete career change to do something more fulfilling.

Stop and think. As you go through your day, stop every now and then to check what thoughts are running through your mind. Are you thinking about how much weight you have put on recently or about the recent break-up with your partner?

Change the spin on those negative thoughts as soon as you spot them, replacing them with something more positive like, "Ok, I've put on weight but I intend to lose those pounds again," or, "that relationship just wasn't meant to be. I'll find someone else who is more suited to me."

Stick with positive people. Surround yourself with people who emit positive vibes rather than grumpy pessimists who will only wear you down. Positive people will uplift you and encourage you to go for your dreams rather than throw a wet blanket on them. Remember that positivity rubs off, so absorb as much of it as you can.

Believe in yourself. Instead of holding on to past failures, insecurities, or painful memories, change your narrative. Life is in the here and now, not in the past, and your future can be bright. Believe that it is possible and let nothing stop you from realizing your dreams.

The Universe and you

You may have heard the expression, "The Universe works in mysterious ways," and in many cases, it does. But, thanks to scientific breakthroughs in the field of quantum physics, we now understand a lot more about the Universe and its energy.

As I said earlier, the law of attraction is an ancient concept with its origins in universal laws. All religions talk about how the Universe was created, and what it is, albeit through different stories and interpretations. They all also ask their followers to 'believe' or to have 'faith' in a supreme power, deity, or consciousness.

For many centuries, philosophers, thinkers, and great minds have devoted their lives to trying to understand how we can fully grasp these ideas and science has always followed suit. Now, as we make more and more discoveries about energy and matter, we are beginning to understand a lot of the ancient wisdom handed down to us. One of the pioneers of quantum physics, Max Planck, once said:

"As a man who has devoted his whole life to the most clear-headed science, to the study of matter, I can tell you as a result of my research about the atoms this much: There is no matter as such! All matter originates and exists only by virtue of a force which brings the particles of an atom to vibration and holds this most minute solar system of the atom together...

We must assume behind this force the existence of a conscious and intelligent Mind. This Mind is the matrix of all matter."

But what does this have to do with the law of attraction? The intelligent Mind Planck refers to is what we can also call infinite consciousness or the Universe, which we are all a part of. This being the case, we all have the ability to influence the world around us by using our energy.

Think about the power of prayer, the power of faith, or the power of meditation, and you will see what I mean. All of them can heal, bring clarity, establish calm, and help us to solve problems.

How can you use your positive energy?

The law of attraction can bring abundance into your life because it hears you, reacts to your positive energy, and responds in kind.

You may be asking how this is possible. We all resonate energy, just in the same way that every atom resonates its own energy. Our energy is electrical (impulses) and chemical (reactions), with our brain using up an estimated 20 percent of the body's energy supply.

We exchange energy with our surroundings every minute of the day and on death, our atoms are repurposed. In other words, we become one with the Universe again and our consciousness continues to echo through space and time. When you think of it like that, you can understand the amazing potential we have to bring our dreams to reality.

Your thoughts are made up of energy that resonates on a certain frequency, just as everything else in the Universe does.

This applies to your feelings and desires too and, according to the law of attraction, vibrational energy resonates with similar vibrational energy. Negative vibes resonate on a low frequency so if you emit them, you will attract negative vibes back. Positive thoughts travel on a higher vibrational frequency, and they are the ones you need to emit if you want to attract abundance in your life.

Your way of thinking and approach to life determines those vibrational frequencies, so it's up to you to raise the vibrations with positive thoughts, qualities, and actions. But you also have to believe in the power to transform your life in this way as it won't work if you just pretend to be happy or pay lip service to the idea.

It really requires a complete transformation on your part and a genuine decision to embrace the concept. You can manifest your wishes when you take action to bring them about by using the right energy.

You also have to stick with it. Trying to think positive for only a day isn't going to get you very far. Like I said earlier on, the law of attraction isn't a quick fix to your problems. It's more like a way of life that you have to practice and apply regularly if you want to see any results. You can nurture positivity by removing negative self-talk, being kind to others, showing generosity and love – all of which will resonate out to the Universe.

If you want to manifest more money in your life, thinking of dollar bills isn't going to be effective. You need to focus on the positive things that having more money will bring and raise your vibrations. Here are some simple ways to do just that:

1. **Put out high-frequency energy**

High-frequency energy is aligned with the higher truths or virtues that we recognize as part of our humanity. These truths are things like love, generosity, gratitude, appreciation, openness, acceptance, kindness, compassion, trust, forgiveness, surrender, happiness, encouragement, inspiration, creativity, contentment, harmony, balance, and flow.

When you begin to practice more of these truths, you will begin to experience more shifts in your life towards positive outcomes. Don't focus on what you can get out of it, but see what you can give to others instead. This is the highest form of energy

2. Break free from whatever is restricting you

Remove anything in your life that you feel is holding you back with its negativity. Perhaps you need to move house, change jobs, get out of a toxic relationship, or practice more self-care.

If you have read my book, **Love Yourself Deeply**, you will recall how I talk a lot about separating yourself from anything negative in life that is preventing you from growing as a person. It's extremely difficult to think positive thoughts if you are caught up in a negative environment and the sooner you change that, the better.

3. Be curious about life

Open up to new adventures, challenges, and experiences, all of which will fill you with positive energy. Tap into your creative side and spend time doing what you love, rather than being preoccupied with obligations. Dance when you feel like it, sing as much as you want to, go barefoot, have a picnic, play games, design something, read more, meet new people.

Basically, do anything that will help you to feel free, childlike, and open to new experiences in life. This keeps your energy frequency high because you are living in the moment and enjoying everything in a carefree manner.

4. Give without expecting anything in return

The act of giving to others is almost a sacred gesture that will come back to you in turn. It doesn't have to be in the form of financial help, but can be as simple as a kind word or a smile.

Give from the heart without expecting to receive credit for your actions, public recognition, or monetary rewards. Just be nice because you can, showing kindness, generosity, and thoughtfulness in any way possible. Don't do it from a sense of guilt or obligation – those intentions resonate on a low frequency – but do it because you truly want to.

5. Be in the moment

This means being conscious of what you do, say, and think. It's a technique known as mindfulness that can help you to really understand where your negative thoughts are coming from, what triggers them, and how you can dismiss them. When you feel angry, for example, instead of letting that feeling escalate, stop and focus on what is happening. Ask yourself, "Why am I really angry? What purpose does my anger serve? How will it affect my inner harmony and well-being?"

When you take time out to ask these questions, not only will you learn something about yourself, but you will also be able to divert that negative energy to something more positive and beneficial. Being present in the moment is key to directing positive energy and avoiding the impact of negativity.

If you really want to manifest more money in your life, you will achieve that once you begin to resonate on a higher energetic level. The potential of the Universe to give you what you ask for is limitless and you have the power to make it happen. That power lies within your mind and in the next chapter, we are going to explore how to tap into that infinite source of potential wealth.

You have the power to create any future that you choose to attract. When you practice the law of attraction, do not doubt that the Universe will respond to you!

Key Points:

- *Follow the 3 rules of the law of attraction to receive abundance.*

- *There is no quick fix or magic wand without positive action.*
- *Your thoughts have the power to transform your life.*
- *Optimistic people emit higher energy frequencies than pessimists.*
- *We are connected with the Universe on every level of existence.*
- *By raising your vibrations, you can manifest your desires.*

4

MANIFESTING MONEY - THE ULTIMATE POWER

"In fact, reality is nothing but waves of possibility that we have "observed" into form." — Pam Grout

You're probably reading this book because you are tired of having a lack of money in your life, or you would like to make more of it. Ironically, you are already breaking the Law of Attraction by having that mindset.

If you remember what we talked about earlier on, negativity attracts negative outcomes, so they may be a very good reason why you aren't enjoying more abundance. Your fixation on 'not having enough money' or desperately wishing you had more implies that you are focusing on scarcity. This is one of those negative thoughts that will not bring a positive outcome because it isn't in line with the principles of the Law of Attraction. Only if you have a positive mindset about money can you create or attract more of it.

So, what you need to do is rewire your thoughts, your words, and your feelings about money. Then, your actions will be more aligned with receiving it.

The truth is that most of us are locked into a negative mindset when it comes to our lives. We constantly relive painful past memories in our minds, recall all of our failures, and wake up each day weighed down by the same problems that we had yesterday. It's not something that we do on purpose, but more of a bad habit and, like all habits, it can be changed if you know how to go about it.

Why am I stuck in a negative cycle?

I want to answer that by talking a little bit about how our brain works. You probably already know that things called neurons are responsible for processing and storing information in our brain. When firing up, they form neural pathways, creating a network of information that jumps via one synapse or junction to the other. The more information our brains connect, the more synapses are formed, giving us the incredible potential for development and growth.

What you may not realize is how positive and negative thoughts affect these super neurons and their synaptic junctions. Yes – positive and negative thoughts really do affect our brain and how we feel. That's because each thought releases a certain kind of chemical. Positive thoughts trigger the feel-good hormone known as serotonin, and negative thoughts release the stress hormone we call cortisol. The higher the levels of serotonin, the less cortisol is produced.

We've all experienced the power of positivity in our lives at some point – those feelings of happiness, contentment, joy, and optimism. When we are in this positive state, it also changes our perception, helps us to be more aware of our own thoughts, increases our attention span, and helps us to think faster.

On the other hand, negative thoughts raise our stress levels, drawing away precious metabolic energy from the prefrontal cortex, which controls things like attention, impulse inhibition, prospective memory, and cognitive flexibility.

Basically, we block our brain from functioning properly, it can't take in information correctly, and everything becomes a bit chaotic. If you've ever been in a state of panic or fear, you will know exactly what I mean. That phrase, "My mind went blank" isn't so far from the truth, as we struggle to "get our thoughts together" and decide what to do.

The more you focus on negativity, the more synapses and neurons you will create to support that negative thought process. We then get stuck in a negative cycle because our brain has been hardwired to recall negative experiences and emotions from our past. In turn, these affect the expectations we have about our future.

Having a hard time when younger or undergoing a painful past experience has such an impact on us that we often feel trapped by those memories. We relive them over and over again, each time reinforcing them so they control how we think and feel about our lives.

I'm going to give you some examples of how that works below:

Event Born poor

Belief - I'll always be poor

Event Lost your job

Belief - I'll never be successful

Event Suffered a trauma

Belief - I'll never be happy

Event Experienced a break-up

Belief I'll always fail at relationships

It's not difficult to see how this mechanism works, and I'm sure that you can think of examples around your own cycle of negative thinking.

In reality, people who are optimists are usually more successful in life, while pessimists tend to have less emotional, motivational, and cognitive balance, which sabotages their ability to succeed.

The good news is that what we say, do, and think affects our brain, so we can retrain it to be more positive by thinking happy thoughts.

How will this help me to manifest more money?

Once we begin to adopt a more positive mentality, it is possible to manifest what we want. This occurs thanks to another chemical produced in the brain called dopamine, which controls the sensations of pleasure we receive when the brain is stimulated by achievement.

When you do achieve something, you get a rush of dopamine and feel good. The brain makes a note of that and would like to give you that feeling over and over again. But if your desires are frustrated, you are starved of dopamine, which leads to fear and anxiety instead.

The trick here is to visualize that you have already attained your goals even if you haven't. By putting yourself into this imaginary scenario, and the feeling of elation that goes along with it, a part of our brain is tricked into thinking we have already achieved it in reality. In effect, it 'believes' that the desired outcome is a real experience and because it likes that dopamine rush, it sets up the conditions for you to actively work towards that goal.

That's why the power of visualization is one of the most potent abilities we have. When we imagine the feeling of getting rich, the brain doesn't know the difference between myth and reality. It simply responds to the 'imagined' emotion of feeling wonderful, releasing dopamine and self-generating that motivation to achieve more. That's why you need to understand how your thinking can bring about all your goals.

Remember:

Negative thoughts lead to:

- Slow brain coordination
- Difficulty in processing thoughts or finding solutions
- Less creative ability
- An increase of the fear factor, affecting mood, memory, and impulse control

Positive thoughts lead to:

- An increase in synapses
- An increase in mental productivity
- Improved ability to pay attention and focus
- Improved ability to think and analyze data
- Improved ability to solve problems more quickly and increase creativity

When you begin to think more positively, you are allowing your brain to respond in turn. After a while, this becomes the norm and you will feel more driven to pursue your goals and even more convinced that you will achieve them.

Thinking positively isn't just some wishy-washy instagram quote, but is a dynamic process that can turn your life into the one you want. Your thoughts become actions and your actions will bring you success. It's that simple!

Imagining your future

Every successful person in the world began by imagining what kind of future they wanted. They didn't rely on luck or chance but had a clear vision of where they wanted to be and then made a plan to achieve that.

When people talk about the law of attraction, it's often misrepresented as some new-age wishful thinking that has no real scientific basis. If you think it can be used to manifest wealth out of thin air without any effort, then you haven't understood it properly. The law refers more to projecting positivity in order to receive it back, which involves more than just saying things like, "I wish I was rich. I wish I had a million dollars in my bank account. I wish all my financial worries were solved." It's not like having a genie in a bottle at all!

There's a little thing called the 'endowment effect' that I want to tell you about. Another way of describing it that you may recognize is when someone tells you to 'own it'. This basically means that when we take ownership of an object or idea, it becomes integrated into our sense of identity. When we feel that we are losing it, this dampens down our dopamine, which is the reward hormone.

If you have set your heart on that new coat you saw in the shop window last week, for example, you already feel like it belongs to you, even though you haven't bought it yet.

Buying it will simply verify that it's yours in reality, while your brain has been believing all along that you already 'own' it. That's why you feel such a flood of disappointment when you return to the shop a few days later, only to learn that it has been sold to someone else.

The interesting thing here is that researchers have discovered the endowment effect doesn't actually require 'real' ownership or even possession of an object. It's sufficient to believe that you will have a reasonable expectation of possessing it in the future to get those dopamine hits spiking.

When we already imagine we have ownership of something, our brain believes us. In the same way, by believing that we will have more money in the future and recognizing how that would make us feel, we are signaling to the brain that we've already achieved it.

To get to that point, we need to set goals and act as if we have already nailed them. No matter how large or small that goal is, an area of our brain wants to attain it in order to help us define who we are.

It will set up the conditions that motivate us to work towards achieving those goals, i.e. by producing dopamine. The brain feels good when it thinks it's accomplished what it set out to do. Bearing this in mind, even if that goal is out there and waiting to be achieved in the future, we can work towards manifesting it in the present.

Using the present to realize your future

The words you use have a massive impact on how you feel, and we are going to go over that subject a little later on. But before that, I want you to look at 3 steps that can change your thoughts each day until you have mastered the art of being in a positive state of mind.

Notice

How often do you stop to check what you are thinking? Contrary to what you may believe, thoughts aren't just random particles floating around in our heads. They are repeated patterns that we have wired our brain to create over and over again. When they are negative, or mainly negative, all they are doing is making you feel bad, useless, hopeless, and incapable of achieving anything.

There are no shots of dopamine or serotonin to bail you out so your thoughts actually have a negative effect on how you feel, even physically. Once you begin to notice these negative thought patterns, you can build a new habit of getting away from that negativity and nurturing more useful mind states.

Shift

When you wake up in the morning and feel inclined to think about what went wrong yesterday, last week, or last year, you are reinforcing negativity. Instead of doing that, bring your attention to your past wins and strengths, focussing on the good times you have experienced and the amazing possibilities awaiting you in the future. Be mindful of when you slip into self-doubt, anxiety, and fear. Stop yourself from conjuring up the worst-case scenario and imagine the best possible outcomes instead.

A good way to enhance this process is by expressing gratitude for the present moment. It may sound like a waste of time, but if you can sit down and give thanks for at least one thing in your life right now, you are creating new neural pathways without even realizing it. Give gratitude for your health, your family, your job, your determination, or whatever comes into your mind.

Rewire

It only takes 15 seconds to form a new mindset and rewire it into your neural pathways. That's incredible, isn't it? By simply savoring those positive thoughts and emotions, you are helping to boost creativity and enter a state of happiness. Your brain will respond in turn as soon as you do this, helping you to look forward to future challenges with a new sense of optimism. Try it once a day for a week and see what happens!

You may find it easy to think happy thoughts but just can't do that when it comes to imagining you will have more money.

This is probably due to the limiting beliefs you have acquired on the subject over the years.

I mentioned this in the chapter about having a 'poverty mindset', which is just one of the ways in which we screw up our relationship with money. The law of attraction requires you to let go of such limiting beliefs and see money from a different perspective.

What is money?

That's a good question, and you will certainly have an opinion on what money means to you. Perhaps you associate it with a means to achieving happiness, or the solution to all of your problems.

Money is basically a resource we can use in any way we wish. The lack or scarcity of it usually makes us feel frustrated and unhappy. Just thinking about not having money, or enough money, can bring us down and prevent us from doing anything to change the situation.

What if I tell you that you have just inherited 10,000 dollars. How would you feel? Elated, ecstatic, overwhelmed, excited? Even imagining that you own more money suddenly brings a smile to your face, and that's the feeling you need to hold on to.

When the law of attraction states that positives will attract positives, it's saying that your energy will resonate on a higher frequency and invite abundance into your life. So even though you may not have really inherited the above sum, imagine how you would feel if you did.

Anyone can make money. All you need to do is set your goals, believe that you will achieve them, and think about how amazing that will feel. How much money you want to make depends on your circumstances. You may just want enough to get by or perhaps you are determined to become a millionaire.

It's not the amount that is important, but the intention behind it, which is why you should see money as a resource and not just a piece of paper or figure in your bank account. It's a means to an end, not an end in itself. When you understand that and begin to put out those positive vibes, the Universe will respond. It's a natural law that can't work in any other way.

Associate money with opportunities for growth or for helping others, rather than thinking of it as wealth that you intend to horde or waste. Think of the gifts you would give to your loved ones or the causes you could support financially instead of planning to spend it all on a weekend in Las Vegas.

Removing money blocks

Many of us want to make more money but have a love-hate relationship with it. There's a lot of negativity attached to money and even more directed at those who have a lot of it.

You need to remove these blocks if you want to invite abundance and wealth into your life. Think about the following statements and place a tick next to the ones that reflect your views on money:

Rich people are greedy

Poor people are helpless

Money corrupts you

Hard-earned money is honorable

Quick money is dirty money

Having a lot of money is sinful/unethical

Money is the root of all evil

If you ticked any of the above statements, spend some time to think about where those opinions come from. Does money corrupt everyone? Are rich people really greedy? I think that if you ponder on it for a while, you will reach the conclusion that all of the above statements are very clearly untrue.

Money does corrupt sometimes, but not always. Some rich people are stingy, but so are some of those people with less. It's not immoral to have a lot of money, and neither is it shameful to experience a lack of it.

Of course, obtaining money by illegal or unethical means is not something I advocate, but not everyone has accumulated wealth by doing so. There are many good, giving people out there who have worked hard to fulfill their dreams of making money. Giving some of your money away not only helps others but will also accrue more for you in the long run because being generous brings abundance.

At the end of the day, it's not about having money, but about what you do with it. Money can make you rich, but if you don't appreciate the good it can bring into your life, then you will never achieve it.

This is the law of attraction, which equates wealth with freeing you from limitations rather than being a slave to your bank balance.

Freeing yourself from limitations

The beliefs that you have about money are most likely holding you back from making more. They won't allow you to reach your dreams, improve your life, or enable you to experience fulfillment. You may often ask yourself why you aren't earning more, or can't find a job, or are failing in business.

Have you ever considered the fact that you are limiting yourself in your approach to making more money by continuing the same habits, behaviors, and thought patterns? The way you see money is directly related to your limiting money mindset, so this needs to go. Here are some suggestions for a new mindset:

Do what you love. You can do what you love and make money. In fact, this is the most productive way to do so. If you feel stuck in a dead-end job, you probably need to find something else that engages, inspires, and motivates you.

Once you do so, you will flourish and find it a lot easier to let go of the negative thought patterns related to work and accumulating wealth. Passion leads to profit, while misery leads to unhappiness and negative vibes.

Rethink the time-money model. Most of us have accepted the idea that we are paid for our time, whether that be an hourly wage or a monthly salary. If you want to make more money using this model, you have to work more hours. How about working fewer hours and making more money than you could ever have imagined?

Many entrepreneurs understand this mindset and focus on smart ways to earn a living. Passive income, side-hustles, and outsourcing are just some of the ways in which successful people handle their valuable time, allowing them to earn even when on vacation.

Estimate your self-worth. How much do you deserve to be paid? Is your salary acceptable to you or do you believe you should be earning more? Whatever you think you are worth, that's what you'll get paid because you accept the deal from the kick-off.

As a businesswoman with years of training behind me and a wide range of skills, I would only be undermining my worth if I charged the bottom dollar for my services. Instead, I charge what I think I am worth and revise that figure often because

I know my worth increases over time. You often get what you ask for, and if you feel worthy of more, strive to reach a figure that allows you to work the same amount of hours (or even less) and improves your quality of life.

Stop equating money with greed. We all know about the cultural stereotype of the fat, rich person who cares little for those poorer than himself. We equate having a lot of money with miserly fictional characters like Scrooge or evil leaders stocking up on gold bars while their people are starving. Let me tell you now: Money can be used to achieve great things and it's how you use it that counts.

You can invest in start-ups, help those in need, sponsor a worthy cause, offer scholarships, or anything that inspires you. When you receive money from the Universe, show your appreciation by sharing it with others. Many financially successful people do this but don't shout about it so you never hear of their kind acts.

Don't rely on luck. You aren't likely to become wealthy by winning the lottery or becoming an overnight success. Most good things in life take time and perseverance and making money is no different. You must take control of your future and not leave it to chance – the chances are, you won't get anywhere. How likely are you to have a windfall, make a million in a competition, or hit the jackpot? By all means, buy those lottery tickets, but don't stake your whole life on winning. You are accepting that you have no control over your destiny, which just isn't true.

Most wealthy people didn't get to where they are today by chance or luck. They did it by being consistently proactive, working hard, and creating opportunities for themselves.

Money can buy happiness. Despite what we are brought up to believe, that material wealth can't buy happiness, it can help us to do so. Having a lot of money (whatever 'a lot' means to you) doesn't imply that you become ecstatic, blissful, and content, but it can give you a nudge in that direction.

It allows you to pay for the resources you need to create a good life for yourself and others. That's a priceless feeling and a wonderful achievement. It can buy you the choices and freedom needed to enable you to do the things that will make you happy. It can bring you financial stability and a reduction in stress, allowing you to enjoy a good life for yourself. This, in turn, will enable you to experience happiness without having to sacrifice your quality of life or worry that you are letting people down.

Build on success in your business. A lot of people are put off from going into their own business because they think they need to invest a substantial amount of capital. In reality, we know this isn't always necessary. Many 'home garage' projects have turned into global enterprises with very little initial outgoings or cash, such as Apple, Hewlett Packard, Amazon, Google, and Mattel.

If you can successfully balance your incomings and outgoings while prioritizing profit, you will always be profitable. When you are ready to expand and grow, there are many ways to do this organically, without massive investment or risk-taking.

Mind your language

I've mentioned negative self-talk a few times, and when it comes to making money, the words you utter or think have much more impact than you probably thought possible.

There are certain words and phrases that you should NEVER use because when you do, you attract negative energy. The law of attraction doesn't pick and choose about what it responds to – it simply works according to the principles of like attracts like. Your words are loaded with energy, inviting whatever it is you are expressing into your life.

Negativity brings negative outcomes, so if you are always complaining about having no money or being broke, unfortunately, that's the energy you will attract. A financially successful person will be thankful for their wealth, attracting even more money, while someone expressing their discontentment at not having money will resonate that and receive more of the same.

If you are suffering from a lack or scarcity of money, you probably think and say things like:

- I'm always broke
- I can't afford to live
- I never have any/enough money
- Money is always tight
- I'll never get rich
- I'm no good with money
- Money will always be a problem

Most of the time, our negative responses are full of words like can't, always, and never. It's almost as if we are declaring that the situation we find ourselves in is unchangeable. Of course, if you believe that's the case, then you will find it extremely difficult to bring about any change because you aren't giving the Universe the chance to share abundance with you.

If you want to become a money magnet, you have to stop giving out negative vibes through your thoughts and feelings. Instead of moaning about your lack of money, use statements like these instead:

- I'm going to attain money very soon
- My life will soon be full of abundance

- I'm grateful for my health/family/job
- I am ready to pursue my dreams
- I will enjoy wealth in my life
- Money is coming my way

Remember that your thoughts are not truths – they are stories you have made up based on your negative experiences. Replace them with a new vocabulary that is full of optimism and positivity as you look to your future. It will get brighter because the Universe always works in your favor when you ask it to.

Now that we've looked at how you can manifest more money in your life, the following chapters will give you specific strategies to put your plans into action. We'll take a look first at the art of visualization and learn how to practice it on a daily basis.

Rather than saying, 'seeing is believing', visualization invites you to believe in something before it actually materializes. You can do this by opening your mind's eye, and that's what we're going to do next.

Key Points:

- *Your brain is wired on a negative cycle.*
- *Positive thoughts reinforce positive neural pathways.*
- *Negative thoughts suppress serotonin and dopamine.*
- *We can visualize our future and make it a reality.*
- *Being in the present helps us to shift and rewire our thoughts.*
- *Removing money blocks allows for infinite possibilities.*
- *Our thoughts and words can create negative or positive outcomes.*

5

HOW VISUALIZATION WORKS

"Having a mental snapshot of where you are, where you are going, and what you are moving toward is incredibly powerful." – Sara Blakely

Imagine this... you are sitting on a sandy beach feeling totally relaxed. The waves lap gently onto the shore and you gaze up at the cloudless sky. You are free of worries about money, bills, or debts and simply enjoy the warm sense of success. Can you feel the cool breeze on your face? Lovely, isn't it?

When you visualize such a scene in your mind's eye, you can actually feel your senses reacting to the stimuli: the view, the sounds, the sensations... that's how powerful your mind is. It's no wonder that visualization techniques like this have been used for years by therapists and health professionals to help get their patients into a calm, relaxed, stress-free state. Perhaps you practice this kind of relaxation yourself and are aware of its benefits.

But visualization techniques can also be used to achieve whatever you want in life, according to the law of attraction. This is because your thoughts consist of energy, as we have already discovered. When you send this energy out, you are telling the Universe exactly what you want, and it will respond with similar energy vibrations. The great thing about visualization is that you can create an exact image of what you want to achieve for your future and see it manifest itself in reality.

It may sound too good to be true, but the power of visualization is used by millions of people, and athletes are a very good example of that. From Olympic judo champions to world-class soccer players, visualizing that medal or winning shot helps them to achieve their ambitions and sports coaches know this too. Many professional coaches get their teams or players to visualize success repeatedly until they feel that they have already won, and a lot of prominent athletes openly talk about how useful visualization has been to them on their path to success.

The facts are there to back it up, too. Research shows that there seems to be a strong overlap of the neuromotor and neurosensory pathways used when actually performing an action, and during a well-performed visualization.

A study carried out by Russian scientists prior to the 1980 Olympics involved dividing athletes up into four groups and delivering specific training to each one. The program was designed like this:

- Group 1: 100% physical training
- Group 2: 75% physical training, 25% mental training
- Group 3: 50% physical training, 50% mental training
- Group 4: 25% physical training, 75% mental training

Surprisingly enough, it was Group 4 that performed the best during the Olympic Games, giving credibility to the idea that when we create a mental picture of what we want to achieve, that can be even more effective than our physical ability to do so.

Since then, many athletes have adopted this kind of training, whether that's imagining themselves flying through the air in a record-breaking ski jump or netting that all-important goal in the World Cup. What they are doing is visualizing their goals in their mind, which helps them to achieve success in real life.

This kind of creative visualization has many uses and you don't need to be an Olympic athlete to enjoy its full benefits. It can improve your health, reduce stress, heal illnesses, and contribute to pain management. It also leads to better cognitive performance, increased self-esteem, and, of course, the achievement of your goals.

There are different types of visualization techniques, and not all of them are confined to your mind's eye. We can create mental images inside our heads or real images through what's known as a vision board (sometimes called a dream board). Both reflect your goals and send out a positive message to the Universe about what you want to achieve.

How does visualization work?

All it takes is for you to create a mental image in your mind of any perceived aspect of the physical world. Using all of your senses, you will be able to smell, taste, see, hear, and touch whatever you like. If you want to conjure up an image of an ice cream, for instance, not only can you see it in your mind, but you can sense holding it in your hand, feel the anticipation of eating it, and notice the chill in your mouth as you taste it.

While you are 'enjoying' your ice cream, your brainwave activity and biochemistry change, with your brain thinking that you really ARE eating an ice cream. Imagine the results if you envision that you have amassed a large sum of money...

What a sublime experience! Just by creating an image of yourself in the future as successful and prosperous, you will feel different, as your thoughts enhance your mood. And while you are in that positive state of mind, you are radiating positive energy to the Universe and will attract that positivity back.

Whatever you visualize, your neurons interpret the image as real and communicate with each other to enable it. Let's say you visualize running through a forest: an impulse will be generated to perform that movement and even though you are still sitting down, the 'new' memory of you doing that action will be stored as a memory.

It's not about pretending that something exists in a fantasy world, but rewiring your brain to 'believe' in this new state of being. So, how can this help you if you want to manifest more wealth?

Why visualization works

Visualization works by helping you to create your dream life – the life where all your goals are attainable. It does so in a number of ways:

It strengthens your motivation to succeed. When you are motivated, you are much more likely to pursue your dreams of making more money.

It programs your brain to believe you have already achieved your goals. When you create an image of something, you enable the brain to believe you have already succeeded in obtaining it.

It gives your brain the chance to figure out how to manifest your goals in the future. Going over something in your head leads you to visualize any possible obstacles in the way. Think of it as a mental rehearsal for what is to come.

It impacts many cognitive processes in the brain: motor control, attention, perception, planning, and memory, all of which create the drive you need to realize your goals.

It makes you feel more confident. When you frequently visualize your goals, you will become more confident about your abilities to achieve them.

Visualization helps you to feel calm. When you visualize, you normally enter a calm state, which helps you to remove any clutter and focus on your specific goal worry-free.

Imagine an artist, who wants to create a masterpiece on canvas. They have a picture in their head of what they want to paint, and carefully craft it into reality with the strokes of a brush.

This is visualization at work and when you apply it to the law of attraction, the possibilities are endless. You can accumulate all the wealth you desire simply by visualizing that you already have it.

Different kinds of visualization

There are two main kinds of visualization that can be used separately, or together for greater effect. The first kind is known as **outcome visualization,** which requires that you envision yourself achieving your desired goal. The second is known as **process visualization,** which involves envisioning the steps you need to take to reach your desired outcome.

Both types of visualization are most successful when you use a multi-sensory approach, sometimes called holistic imagery. You can hold an image in your mind's eye or a physical image, such as a photo, and the more vivid the image is, the more profound its effect on your mind. As you imagine your goal, summon up the emotions you will likely feel, as well as the aromas, the sounds, the sensations – anything that your senses can pick up.

For **outcome visualization**, you need to create a detailed mental image of actually experiencing your dream coming to fruition by incorporating all of your senses. If, for example, your goal is to make your first million in twelve months, close your eyes and imagine that you have already succeeded.

Envision yourself having a celebratory dinner in a fancy restaurant and notice the sense of joy and exhilaration. Listen to the fizz of the champagne as it pours into the fine crystal glass between your fingertips. Savor the wonderful meal you are enjoying with friends and loved ones and toast to your success. Retaining this virtual experience in your mind will actually make your brain believe it is already a done deal.

For **process visualization**, focus on each action or milestone that you need to reach as you work towards your final goal. You aren't concerned so much about the outcome itself, but more about what you need to do to get to the finish line. You may find it useful to write your goals down or even draw a chart, a diagram, or pictures of them – whatever works for you.

If you use this method intending to make your first million, create the steps that you need to act upon to make it happen. For example, your first milestone may be to sell your house and invest the profit. Imagine in your mind's eye that you have already found a buyer and are signing the sale contract. Notice the pen you are holding in your hand gliding along the paper as you sign your name and sense the excitement of having achieved this first step on your path to success. What a feeling!

Visualizing your life goals

Everyone can master the art of visualization and improve their quality of life. It doesn't require any special skills, nor do you need to have any intense training. You can use visualization for short-term or long-term goals and with practice, you will become even more proficient at it.

When you see the results, you will also be even more convinced that you can manifest your goals of making more money and accumulating greater wealth.

There are several ways to practice visualization, such as meditation, vision boards, and creative visualization. Affirmations and journaling are also powerful ways to ask the Universe for what you want, and I'll talk more about them in a later chapter. For now, let's look at some of the techniques you can use to make your dreams a reality by aligning your energy with the law of attraction.

Goal-oriented meditation

If you've never tried meditation before, don't worry. Although the practice has its roots in ancient eastern philosophies, you don't need to change your belief system, faith, or religion. Think of it more like quiet contemplation or reflection, in which you simply relax for a few moments and turn your focus inward. You can meditate at home, on your commute to work, in a park, or anywhere you feel is suitable.

The main thing is to find a comfortable place to sit and start to think about a goal you wish to accomplish. If you want to make $10,000 in six months, for example, state that as your intention. Begin to visualize how it feels to have reached your target. Imagine yourself in that future place and call to mind any sensations you expect to feel... all the positive vibes, the contentment, satisfaction, and sense of achievement. Allow yourself 10 minutes to stay in this state of 'achievement' before finishing your meditation practice.

If you do this every day, it will soon become a healthy habit. You can use goal-oriented meditation to achieve anything you want in life, as long as you believe in the power of your thoughts.

Here's an example of the kind of goal-oriented meditation I practice when I want to achieve something specific in my life:

1. Make yourself comfortable and close your eyes.

2. Take a deep breath in and exhale slowly. Continue to do so throughout the meditation.

3. Begin by focusing in your mind on a particular aspect of your life.

4. Now, start to imagine the highest possible outcome you would like to reach in 3 to 6 months from now.

5. Choose a goal that is meaningful and special to you. Make it something so significant that, once you achieve it, you will feel wonderful and even motivated to set your next goal.

6. Make sure it is specific, measurable, achievable, realistic, and time-defined (SMART).

7. Now that you have honed in on your goal, imagine living the life you envision once you achieve it, free from any limitations or negativity. Create a picture in your mind and place yourself inside this visual as if you are really there. Where are you? Who is there with you? What is happening around you?

8. Next, step out of the image you've created and imagine floating back to where you are now, taking a mental picture with you of your achieved goal.

9. As you continue to inhale and exhale, imagine yourself floating into the future and see yourself in the place you wish to be in 3 or 6 months' time.

10. Visualize your achievement and notice how you feel about it.

11. Slowly drift back to the present and consider what actions you need to take over the next few weeks or months to get closer to your goal.

12. Before you open your eyes, take a few more deep breaths, letting go of all worry and stress as you do so.

13. Now you are ready to take action with every day that follows, keeping the vision of your achievement clear in your mind's eye.

If you find this practice too difficult to do on your own, there are hundreds of useful goal-oriented guided meditations available on online platforms like YouTube and Spotify that you can use. In these audio transcripts and videos, a narrator will walk you through a meditation designed to help you envision your goals so check them out and give them a try until you get the hang of it.

Vision boards

Do you remember making collages when you were younger? I used to make them often, filling mine with all kinds of bits and pieces. As a memento of my summer holidays with my family, for instance, I once made a collage on a large piece of cardboard which I hung on my wall. It was full of things like tickets to the funfair, funny photos, chocolate wrappers, sand from the beach, dried flowers... anything that reminded me of my vacation.

A vision board is similar, but instead of reminding you of a past occasion, it will enable you to imagine a specific time in your future.

Vision boards are powerful visualization tools that you can use to represent your goals and dreams. They can be made up of words, images, or anything else that creates a collage of your future goals. Nowadays, you can make a digital version or use a corkboard and pins. However you do it, the point is to place your vision board somewhere that allows you to view it frequently throughout the day.

Another way that vision boards work is by prompting you to visualize your ideal life or goals regularly, which activates the power of your subconscious mind to manifest what it believes to be true. Your brain makes a blueprint of your envisioned goals and, in line with the law of attraction, you are acting like a magnet that pulls the resources and opportunities to achieve success toward you.

It also increases your motivation, making you more determined to achieve your goals. If, for example, you wish to have enough money to buy a house in the Caribbean, your vision board could be filled with images of your dream house, palm-lined sandy beaches, exotic landscapes, and flight tickets.

When you constantly see your vision board in front of you, you will start to notice you are doing things that move you closer to your goal. You will find yourself thinking of ways to save money, cut back on spending, sell off any property or items of value, and look for a new kind of employment that allows you to earn more, all with the intent of eventually realizing your dream.

Before you make your vision board, consider the following:

What are my goals? Be specific about what you really want and why you want to achieve it.

Who do I need to become to achieve this goal? What changes do you need to make in your life to make your dream a reality? More adventurous? More hard-working?

What help will I need? Who or what can enable me to turn my vision into a reality?

What skills will I need to improve? Is there any particular skill that will help you on your way to achieving your goal? Perhaps take a course about setting up your own businesses or attend a night class to learn a new language...

What stumbling blocks might I face? Consider any obstacles in your way and how you will overcome them.

To create your vision board, you can add your own personal photos, images from the web, or magazine cut-outs – anything that represents your goals and inspires you to pursue your dreams. You can also add bold words, quotes, or statements that capture the essence of what you wish to achieve. Choose words that evoke the feeling you most want to experience in your future plans.

You can use free software like Canva, PicMonkey, or Pinterest to create a digital vision board, which also have massive photo banks and text-formatting tools for you to use to create something specific to your goal. Once you have created your digital vision board, save it and use it as your screensaver on your desktop or wallpaper on your mobile phone.

Every time you look at your screen, take a minute to remind yourself of how good it will be when you reach your goal. Imagine things such as how you will feel, what the temperature will be like, what you are wearing, what aromas you can smell, and so on. The more you visualize your goals and stay focused, the more inspired you will be to take action to achieve them.

How to stay focused

Many people create vision boards and then get frustrated when nothing seems to be changing around them. They find themselves stuck in the same job, still don't have enough money, or their dream of having that new house seems further away than ever. This is because they forget they need to take action in order to achieve their goals. If your vision board represents your new successful business, for example, you need to create a bridge to get you from A to B.

That means you also need to visualize any hurdles you may face on the way. Imagine yourself being unable to get enough investment or not finding the right software for your needs. Place those steps at the forefront of your mind and acknowledge the work ahead of you. By doing so, you will remain focused on your end goal but also have much greater awareness of what is needed to get there without wanting to quit.

Creative visualization

If you want to take your creativity one step further, or are more expressive by nature, you can engage in activities that really help you to envision your goal of buying that new house or making it to millionaire status. You can do so by painting yourself in the future, writing about your new life, or even creating graphics on your computer. Just as you would with a vision board, place your art where you can see it often, and let yourself experience the feeling of having already reached your goal.

Visualization is an extremely powerful tool if you wish to manifest your dreams. It allows you to see how you can change your life, and give you the inspiration and insights to do exactly that. It triggers your determination, motivation, and imagination, emitting all that positivity on a very high frequency out into the Universe.

The law of attraction is always at work in your life and by visualizing your goals regularly, you will soon see them manifesting before your very eyes.

Key Points:

- *Visualization has been proven to bring greater success in all walks of life.*
- *It works by rewiring your brain and enhancing cognitive abilities.*
- *Visualization can be used to achieve short or long-term goals.*
- *Goal-oriented meditation can be practiced anytime, anywhere.*
- *Vision boards are useful tools to inspire and motivate you.*
- *Creative visualization helps you to express your inner desires.*
- *Your vision resonates out to the Universe on a very high frequency.*

6

HOW TO CONNECT THE DOTS

"If you can dream it, you can do it." – Walt Disney

The law of attraction exists, whether you take advantage of it or not. Once you begin to use manifestation techniques in your daily life, you will soon learn how to leverage them to achieve whatever you like. In fact, the more results you see, the more you will wonder why you hadn't tried it before.

It's a gift we can all use, so why not take advantage of it? It does require you to follow some steps and it's not as simple as sitting back and thinking, "I'd like a new sports car." Those who use manifestation techniques know that they have to practice them frequently and truly invest in the belief that their efforts will bear fruit. If you want to manifest your dreams, you have to be prepared to work for them, but the rewards are infinite.

The Law of Manifestation states that we can realize our goals if we focus on them and follow through with supportive action, making it tie in nicely with the law of attraction that claims we receive what we put out. That includes our thoughts, feelings, and beliefs. If you try to manifest a future goal half-heartedly, it isn't likely to work because you are not doing it with genuine commitment. You may say, "I'll give it a try," while your subconscious is telling you that it's not likely to be successful. That's why it's very important to put your whole heart and mind into the process.

Vocalizing any of your goals via affirmations is a further step towards attracting abundance and when you have mastered all these techniques, you can fully leverage the law of attraction to your advantage.

For example, if you want a new car, by thinking about it and visualizing what it will feel like to drive it, you will already have raised your vibrations. When you set goals to achieve your objectives and believe that you can then successfully manifest them, the chances are that you will.

How to improve your manifesting techniques

The first thing you need to do is check your thoughts and feelings for any negativity. Do you have any niggling doubts in the back of your mind? Are you in a bad mood or feel that nothing is going to work out as you would like?

Spend some time to look at where these thoughts and feelings are coming from because if you start out with a negative attitude, it will be difficult to manifest what you really want. Once you are in a positive mindset and have cleared those negative vibrations, there are some useful manifestation techniques you should use every day.

9 bulletproof ways to attract what you want

Think of manifestation techniques as daily rituals that you incorporate into your life. The key is to do each one with an open heart and a willingness to trust the process. Persistence is key here, so think about how you can weave these practices into each day from the moment you wake up.

1. Eliminate self-limiting beliefs

I mention this technique first because if you are stuck in a negative belief cycle, you cannot make any advancement toward your goals. You are literally binding your own hands and feet and need to release yourself from whatever is holding you back. It's not easy to shake off the beliefs you have about yourself and life in general. You may have had a hard time achieving anything and often come down on yourself very harshly. Getting over these impressions of what you can or cannot do, or what you deserve, will enable you to pursue your dreams with much more vigor and optimism.

The 'self-fulfilling prophecy' is a sociological theory often used to describe why some people succeed in life while others fail. More often than not, the ones who fail do so because they never thought they would succeed in the first place. By starting off with that mindset, they do little to help themselves and might even self-sabotage their own chances of success. Of course, when they do fail as a result, they are fulfilling their initial low expectations or prophecy. If you have such a mindset, you need to turn it around. Successful people don't believe they will fail at the outset and never leave the outcome in the hands of destiny or fate. They strive for results and believe in their abilities to succeed.

You can tap into your subconscious beliefs about yourself by practicing mindfulness, which allows you to observe each thought that comes up. View it as if you are a third-person and detach it from who you really are. It's just a thought that has been holding you back and it's time to let it go because you don't need it now. Try practicing mindfulness whenever you notice that your mind is filled with fear, doubt, or hesitation, and you will soon learn to transform your thoughts into more positive ones.

2. Be clear about what you want

If you aren't clear about what you want, how can you achieve it? In order to manifest anything, you need to know exactly what that is and be very specific about your desired outcome. Making sweeping statements such as, "I want to be rich", or "I want to have more money" isn't telling the Universe what you actually want and you aren't going to know how to get it. You need to use the SMART goals that we talked about in the last chapter and make a clear plan of action that will help you to focus. For example, if your desired outcome is to get a high-paying job, sit down and start planning. Outline every detail of how you can succeed, noting things like:

Your skills - list each one.

Your experience - note all of your work experience to date.

Your strengths - list your greatest assets.

Your weaknesses - what do you need to improve upon?

The position of the new job - what would you like to do?

The responsibilities - what responsibilities are you capable of taking on?

The location - will it be nearer or further away from home? Can you work remotely?

The company - do you want to work for a large multi-national or a small family firm?

Work culture - what environment would you be happy working in?

Salary - write down the figure you would like to earn.

Once you have finished your list, place it somewhere that you can refer to it easily and keep looking over it. Add any further details you like and tell yourself that you will land this job by a certain deadline – give yourself a reasonable amount of time to do your research and prepare so you are 100% ready.

Even if you don't succeed, don't let it put you off. Curveballs are often thrown at us in life to make us aware of other options. Sometimes, you need to change plans and you have to trust that the Universe knows what it's doing. Stay aligned with the positivity that it will bring to you by keeping your vibrations high and don't give up.

3. Sensory visualization

Now that you know more about visualization and vision boards, you can practice using sensory stimuli as often as you like. In fact, surround yourself with visual prompts that remind you of your goals as much as you can. To use the example of acquiring that new car, make a vision board of it that you can download to your phone or computer. Stick pictures of the model you want on your fridge and tell yourself it is already yours.

Imagine how the soft leather smells on the seats when you sit inside it, and the feel of the steering wheel between your fingers. Conjure up the sound of the revving of the engine and the sensation of driving smoothly down the highway, feeling as free as a bird. When you involve all of your senses, you create a much more holistic visualization experience, which is channeling all of your energy into manifesting your dream.

4. Word clouds

Everyone knows the power of the written word and when we read, our brain not only believes what it sees, but words also evoke strong emotions in us. In order to use this to your advantage, it's a good idea to create a word cloud, which is basically a cluster of words on a page that have meaning to you. The bigger and bolder the words, the more powerful their impact on your brain, helping you to manifest your goals easily.

You can create your own word cloud by using brightly colored marker pens to write your chosen keywords on a large piece of paper and hang it on your wall or scan it to your pc to use as your screensaver or wallpaper. If you aren't into home crafts, there are some great online apps where you can generate a word cloud such as wordart.com and worditout.com. I created an example in only a few minutes, which you can see below.

You can use inspirational quotes or favorite sayings that remind you of your goal and keep you motivated. Even successful businesses use this technique when wanting to create business plans, brainstorm, and get new ideas. It really does work so why not try it!

5. Focus wheels

Similar to a word cloud, a focus wheel is another useful visual tool and is very easy to create. It will help you to shift your focus from limiting thoughts towards energizing ones that assist in manifesting your dreams.

Simply draw a small circle on paper or a board and write down what you want to achieve. Let's say you write '50,000 dollars'. Next, start jotting down any positive thoughts you associate with your main goal around the circle. For example, you could write phrases like, 'I will save more money', or 'I will make better choices when investing money'. This exercise gets you to hone in on your objective and encourages you to achieve it in practical terms by visualizing your thoughts in black and white.

6. Act as if you have achieved your goal

When kids play make-believe, they really get into that role, forgetting all about reality for a moment. You can do the same thing by acting as if you have already achieved your desired goal and when you get into that mindset, you will begin to believe it is true. Just in the same way that you act full of confidence in a job interview even if you are feeling extremely anxious, you can pretend that you are already living your dream. The feeling it evokes will convince you that you can achieve it, making you even more determined to be successful.

It's useful here to think about why you want to reach your desired outcome: How will it change your life? What rewards will it bring? If you take the new job for example, apart from a higher salary, how will it benefit your well-being? Will it bring you more free time to spend with your family, fewer hours spent commuting, new experiences, or travel opportunities? These possibilities are the things that will evoke more meaning for you and spur you on to reach your desired goal. The universe responds to those positive vibrations by offering more in return so why not fake it until you make it!

7. Stay away from negativity

Apart from your negative thoughts, you could find yourself in situations or environments that get you down and prevent you from feeling positive about life. Even certain people can emit very negative energy, and you need to find ways to avoid these in order to be able to manifest what you really want.

You may know many toxic people in your life who always criticize you or complain about everything. If you spend enough time with people like this, they eventually sap you of all that positivity you need to manifest your dreams, leaving you feeling down, despondent, and emotionally sapped of energy.

It's not easy to remove people from your life, especially if they are family or close friends. But what you can do is restrict the time that you spend with them and explain nicely that you need your space. You don't have to justify why that is and are not obliged to go into detail about your goals for your future. It's your life and if those around you want to support you, great. But if they can't, maintain your positive vibes and remain focused on what you want to achieve without allowing others to sabotage that.

8. Be grateful and practice self-love

Even if you don't see results right off, go easy on yourself. It's not possible to realize all of your dreams overnight and it takes effort and patience. But you can practice gratitude for what you have accomplished so far, even if it's just the fact that you have laid down a plan for how to achieve your goal.

When you are too hard on yourself, you are giving off negative vibrations, and we know where that goes. Resist the temptation to tell yourself things like, "I'll never make it happen," and instead say, "I'm so blessed to be able to pursue my dreams at this stage in my life."

If you practice a daily gratitude ritual and are kinder to yourself, it will prevent you from losing momentum and slumping into bouts of frustration. When you get into the habit of expressing gratitude, you enter the realm of abundance and free yourself from that scarcity mindset. So what if you haven't achieved what you set out to do yet? Rejoice in the fact that you are here and able to work towards reaching your dreams. When you focus on what you have, rather than what you haven't, you are channeling pure, positive energy that will come back to you in time.

In order to practice gratitude on your manifesting journey, you can do the following:

Write down three things you're grateful for every day. It could be your patience, your ability to express yourself well, or your growing confidence.

Before you go to sleep each night, think of one thing that you are grateful for that happened today. Maybe you managed to get a job interview or met an inspiring person at work. Even if it's just a 'thank you' for your good health, being grateful aligns your positive vibes with the Universe.

Take care of your wellbeing by exercising regularly, eating power foods, and treating yourself with a small gift or pampering session. Spend more time with those who mean the most to you in life and soak up the love they feel for you.

9. Keep a manifesting journal

If you like writing down your thoughts, keeping a manifesting journal is a great visualization tool to elevate your vibrational energy and it's easy to do. Use any kind of notebook or create a document on your pc or laptop and as you begin to write regularly, you will find greater clarity about what you want and how to go about it. It will also help you to keep focus and remind yourself of what it is you wish to accomplish instead of getting distracted by other things going on in your life.

The words you write hold power so use positive ones that will fill you with enthusiasm and make you accountable and committed to the process. It's the same as when you tell a friend, "I'm going to buy a new house by the end of the year," which then holds you to doing just that as you wouldn't want them to think you don't follow through.

You can use a journal to express your thoughts and feelings. When you write about yourself, this can give you insights into where you are going wrong, what you need to improve on, and how positive or negative your vibrations really are. Often, it isn't until we write things down that we truly get insights into our own thoughts so journalling will give you the awareness that you need to be more intentional about manifesting what you dream of.

Use a journal to script your desired life story. This is similar to the 'act as if...' in point 6 above. Scripting basically means creating a story about how you envision your life in the future although it is written in the present tense as if you are living it now. Here, all you need is your imagination to describe anything that you have 'achieved' through trusting in the law of attraction. By acting and feeling as if you already have what you want, you will raise those feel-good vibrations and be more likely to achieve your goals.

Create a desire list. You can write down more than one thing you wish to attain in the future. It's perfectly fine to wish for more money, better health, a new house, or whatever you like. The Universe is infinite and the possibilities are limitless so don't restrict yourself to manifesting one solitary thing. The more often you look at your list, the greater chance you have of manifesting your desires. Whenever you reach one of those goals on your list, your faith in the law of attraction will be reinforced as you mark it with a big tick!

Despite practicing some or all of the manifestation techniques above, you may have doubts about their efficacy when you don't see immediate results. This is where you will find it most difficult to trust in the process, but by failing to do so, you will cancel all of your hard work up till now. Instead of dwelling on what hasn't worked out so far, concentrate on the steps you have taken to manifest what you desire and don't let negativity bring you down.

Trust that everything is as it should be and any hurdles or roadblocks are put there for a reason. They could be a test of your determination and resilience, but if you truly want something enough, the Universe will hear you and reply at the right time. Be open to signs from the Universe when practicing manifestation that you would normally put down to coincidence and keep believing that you will attract abundance when everything is correctly aligned.

How long it will take to manifest your dreams depends on what they are. By manifesting them in a number of ways, you are increasing your chances of achieving them and the clearer your vision, the better positioned you will be to achieve success. Choose whatever technique works best for you and use them in any combination, always remembering to do so with gratitude for what you already have in life.

You should also use manifestation affirmations every day, and we'll be talking about their power in the next chapter. Affirmations can eliminate the negativity in your subconscious mind and empower you with positive energy as they rewire your neural pathways so they are definitely a useful tool to help manifest whatever is on your list.

For now, remember that you have the power to achieve anything that you set your mind to. In fact, you are already attracting abundance and can attract more wealth any time you want. It's in your hands!

Key Points:

- *The law of attraction is related to the law of manifestation.*
- *By eliminating self-limiting beliefs, you can achieve your goals.*
- *The clearer your objectives, the more likely the Universe will respond.*
- *Sensory visualization, word clouds, and focus wheels send a direct message to the Universe.*
- *Act as if you have already achieved your goals.*
- *Stay away from negative thoughts, people, or situations.*
- *Maintain a journal to manifest your dreams.*
- *Give gratitude for what you have today and practice self-love.*

7

POWERFUL AFFIRMATIONS TO ATTRACT MONEY TO YOU

"I figured that if I said it enough, I would convince the world that I really was the greatest." – Muhammad Ali

You may have heard of the term 'affirmations' and aren't sure what they are or how useful they can be to you. When we talk about the law of attraction, they are used to reprogram our subconscious mind and remove negativity so that we can attract more abundance.

Affirmations are simple, positive statements that help us to focus our attention on our goals and can also promote self-change from within. By making daily affirmations, it is possible to attract greater wealth, happiness, and even love.

The practice of affirmations began around the 1920s, when they were first made popular by the classic book, Think And Grow Rich, by Napoleon Hill. Nowadays, you will find every lifestyle coach and internet guru encouraging their followers to use affirmations and there is a very good reason for that – they really do work.

Neuroscientists have looked into the changes in the brain while we are making positive self-affirming statements, and have found some surprising results. The evidence after using MRI scans shows how our neural pathways are increased when we make affirmations regularly. (Cascio et al., 2016).

The brain's prefrontal cortex that is involved in positive valuation becomes more active during affirmations, leading to better problem-solving. They can also help to improve our task-related performance, driving us to work towards our objectives. As you know already, attracting what you want from the Universe requires that you take action, and affirmations can give you the motivation you need.

Our subconscious plays a large role in what we believe about ourselves so if we change it to have a more positive outlook, that can significantly impact our ability to pursue our goals. If you tell yourself every day that you are strong enough to meet any challenges, you will really start to believe it after a while.

Apart from increasing your chances of raising your positive vibrations, experts have noticed that affirmations can reduce stress, increase physical behavior that brings greater health benefits, and improved academic achievement. All in all, there's a lot to be said for the practice of affirmations, as well as enabling you to foster a better sense of self as a whole.

Affirmations aren't the same as mantras, which have more spiritual connotations and include sacred words or verses. You don't have to ascribe to any spiritual or religious beliefs with affirmations and anyone can use them as part of their daily ritual.

General positive affirmations to improve your well-being will be short statements such as the ones below:

- I believe in myself and trust my judgment

- I am a successful person
- I am confident and feel good about myself

If you want to use the law of attraction to your advantage, affirmations are a fantastic way to do that because they give you an instant lift, filling you with positive energy that resonates out to the Universe. Positive energy brings positive results, such as financial abundance, fulfilling relationships, and renewed health – anything we desire, actually.

The 7 golden rules for effective affirmations

There is a tried and tested formula for powerful affirmations although it is quite simple and anyone can create their own. Find a quiet place where you won't be disturbed as you craft your affirmations and keep the **7 golden rules** in mind:

1. Make your affirmations short.

They only need to be short statements that are easier to remember and can even be four or five words. It's more important what your intent is rather than how many words you use and the shorter, the better.

2. Write affirmations in the first person.

Affirmations should always begin with 'I', which relate to your identity. Some examples of I statements are, "I am confident in doing my job," "I enjoy looking after my health," and "I am a caring and compassionate person." These are general statements that you feel closely match your identity as a person.

3. Affirmations are always positive.

Your affirmations should always highlight something positive, rather than negative. For example, instead of saying, "I no longer abuse myself with alcohol," you could say, "I am completely free of alcohol," or "I am healthy and make healthy choices for my body."

4. Affirmations should include emotive language.

The more feeling you put into your affirmations, the greater impact they will have on your neural pathways. Emotive words are closely linked to our sense of feeling good so we should use things like, "I love helping others," "I am truly grateful for the abundance in my life," or "I feel wonderful today and full of vitality."

Some positive words you can use are:

Amazed, Appreciated, Confident, Creative, Delighted, Empowered, Enthusiastic, Excited, Focused, Fortunate, Free, Happy, Harmonious, Inspired, Joyous, Loving, Open, Optimistic, Passionate, Positive, Powerful, Proud, Strong, Thankful, Uplifted, Vibrant, Wise, Worthy.

5. Use affirmations to refer to the present.

They should be spoken as if they are happening now rather than expressing future hopes or dreams. This makes the experience much more effective because we really believe that they are describing our present state. Therefore, choose ones that say something like, "I am happy and fulfilled," instead of, "I will be happy and fulfilled this time next year." Putting a time frame on your affirmation limits the time that you have to make it happen so just leave it open-ended instead.

6. Avoid affirmations beginning with "I want" or "I need."

Wanting and needing can reveal a lack of something or scarcity, which is a negative mindset. Instead, create affirmations that express how grateful you are for already having what you want.

7. Don't get caught up in the 'hows'.

Simply affirm something positive, without feeling the need to explain to yourself how you will achieve that. Let your subconscious work that out in good time and make sure they include things you want to realize in the future, rather than just stating any achievements up to now.

How do you use affirmations?

You should make affirmations daily – think of them as recharging your positive energy levels, just in the same way as you would charge your cell phone. Begin by writing down your affirmations, remembering to focus on what you wish to achieve in the future. If you want to generate greater prosperity, for example, create affirmations based on how you will feel when you succeed in doing so. You can create new affirmations every day if you like and the actual act of writing them down helps them to become embedded in the unconscious mind.

Do your affirmations first thing in the morning or last thing at night, or you can even repeat them 4-5 times per day. In fact, the more you utter them, the better, and you can repeat them in front of a mirror to make them even more powerful. Write them on sticky-notes or make affirmation cards that you can place around the house, in your car, in your wallet/purse, or on your desk. These are credit-card-sized pieces of paper with your affirmations on them and you can either create them yourself or purchase ready-made ones online.

There are also many affirmation apps available for your smartphone, which usually come with pre-stocked affirmations relating to health, wealth, and relationships. Some apps, such as ThinkUp, allow you to create more personalized affirmations and can be a great source of inspiration while other apps like Shine send you an SMS message each day with a motivational affirmation to help you fulfill your goals.

If you want to create affirmations that will bring you greater financial abundance, you need to be able to envision the life you want to have when money is no problem. You can begin by asking yourself questions such as:

How would I feel if money was no object?

What would my life look like?

Who would I generously share my wealth with?

Once you have thought about that, you can make affirmations that reflect your future life, free of money worries. In fact, imagine that you have more than enough money and stay with this feeling. You need to believe it is possible and be prepared to work towards that end, with your daily affirmations reflecting all the positivity that having enough money will bring you.

It may seem a bit weird when you first begin making your affirmations but you will soon get used to them. I'm sure you already fill your head with negative self-talk, saying things like, "I'm always broke," "I'm so bad with money," and you know you have convinced yourself that these statements define you. It's time to redefine who you are, with wonderful affirmations that are empowering instead. Just by spending a couple of minutes each day affirming your positivity, you will gradually be able to change your mindset and manifest wealth in your life so enjoy it and savor each moment!

What kind of affirmations do you need?

Depending on your situation, there are different affirmations for different needs. Not everyone is in the same boat, with some people being totally penniless and others earning less than they would like. At the end of the day, you know what your dreams are but one thing you will have in common with everyone else is that you want to attract more money. You might also want to be able to manage your money better and feel like you have greater control. Some of you could want to earn more than you already do or would like to feel comfortable with having money. A lot of folks don't know how to efficiently handle money when they have it and are tempted to waste it, which could be related to the poverty mindset they have developed over the years.

Whichever situation you find yourself in, the basic rules apply to your affirmations. They should be:

- Short
- Personal
- Using the present tense
- Filled with positivity
- Specific enough to visualize
- Contain 'feeling' words
- Spoken or written frequently

Once you get used to making positive affirmations, you will feel more comfortable saying them. An important aspect of affirmations is that they represent your core values so if you have a bad relationship with money, they can help you to overcome that. Their benefits can last for months, eventually forming a positive feedback loop that alters the way you see yourself. When that happens, all of your actions will be closely connected to your prime goals and you will feel more worthy of receiving whatever it is you dream of.

Let's take a look at some affirmations you can use, beginning with some general statements to improve your belief in yourself. After that, you'll find affirmations grouped into various categories, which you can use in any sequence to attract more financial abundance into your life.

I Believe In Myself

20 Powerful affirmations you really need to start telling yourself

1. I am a good person.
2. I am an honest person.
3. I'm a dedicated and loving partner/parent.
4. I am kind and generous.
5. I take care of my health
6. I am beautiful both inside and out.
7. I can achieve anything I set my mind to.
8. I am talented and hard-working.
9. I love who I am and who I'm about to become.
10. I am unique and full of creativity.
11. I am capable of learning a lot.
12. I am brave and persistent.
13. I am worthy of love and respect.
14. I am safe and calm.
15. I trust myself.
16. I am proud of who I am.
17. I believe in myself.
18. I am loved and give love generously.
19. I am strong and determined.
20. I am capable of great things.

Manifesting Money

20 positive affirmations to attract abundance into your life.

1. I am a money magnet and prosperity is drawn to me.
2. I accept and receive unexpected money with gratitude.
3. Money comes to me easily and effortlessly.
4. Wealth flows constantly into my life.
5. My finances get better and better with each passing day.
6. I am joyfully attracting money at this very moment.

7. I welcome all the wealth life brings me with open arms.
8. I attract more money into my life than I could ever have imagined.
9. The more I focus on happiness, the more money I attract.
10. I feel the energy of money flowing through my life.
11. I have the power to attract wealth and money into my life.
12. Money is abundant and unlimited.
13. My thoughts attract wealth and abundance.
14. Everything I need to attract wealth is here right now.
15. Money is all around me and I just have to receive it.
16. People love giving me money.
17. I am aligned with the energy of wealth and abundance.
18. I am so grateful for being able to manifest money.
19. I am creating an abundant future with my thoughts today.
20. I allow prosperity to flow into my life.

Managing Your Finances

20 affirmations to help you successfully manage your abundance.

1. I can overcome any money obstacles that stand in my way.
2. I conquer my money goals with courage and bravery.
3. I am in control of my wealth.
4. I can successfully handle large sums of money.
5. I am excellent at managing my money.
6. I believe in the importance of money.
7. I know that money brings freedom to my life.
8. My ability to grow more money increases every day.
9. I always have more money flowing in than going out.

10. My income is always greater than my expenses.
11. I can manage and invest my money very easily.
12. My finances continue to improve every day.
13. I am enjoying my wealth on my own terms.
14. I use money to change my life for the better.
15. I control money; money doesn't control me.
16. I can tackle all money obstacles.
17. I have the power to improve my relationship with money.
18. I can build the financial future that I desire with hard work.
19. I make hard financial choices with discipline and wisdom.
20. I have control over what I spend.

Earning Money

20 positive affirmations to help you earn more money.

1. Making money comes easily to me.
2. I am deserving of more money.
3. I embrace new ways to increase my income.
4. I welcome an unlimited income into my life.
5. I attract opportunities that create more money.
6. I constantly discover new sources of income.
7. My income is growing higher and higher.
8. I attract more than enough income to support my lifestyle.
9. I earn more money while doing what I love.
10. My bank account is constantly filling up with more money.
11. There are no limits to the amount of money I can make.
12. My income is steadily increasing with each passing day.

13. Money is an abundant source that I continually earn more of.
14. There are no limits to how much I can earn.
15. I welcome the flow of money from multiple sources.
16. I use my skills to bring in more and more money.
17. I believe I am capable of earning more money.
18. I deserve to earn more tomorrow than I make today.
19. Every day is a fresh opportunity to earn more money.
20. I am grateful and respectful of the wealth in my life.

How You Feel About Money

20 affirmations to evoke positive emotions about money.

1. I am grateful for all the money I have.
2. I love money because money loves me.
3. I am worthy of the wealth I desire.
4. I release all negative energy over money.
5. Money brings joy and comfort into my life.
6. I can be a good person and be wealthy at the same time.
7. I am at peace with having a lot of money.
8. I love money and all the goodness it brings into my life.
9. I deserve to have money and be wealthy.
10. I let go of all my limiting beliefs about money.
11. I let go of all my fears around money.
12. I know that everyone can be wealthy, including me.
13. The money I have brings joy to myself and those around me.
14. I attract wealth by being honest and authentic in everything I do.
15. I am worthy of being wealthy, just like everyone else.
16. I am deserving of a prosperous life.
17. I am on the path to a wealthy life.

18. Financial security and freedom bring me peace of mind.
19. I enjoy money and all it offers me.
20. I embrace a life of abundance, wealth, and prosperity.

Using Your Wealth

20 affirmations to help you share your abundance with others.

1. I am generous with my money.
2. I contribute to making the world a better place with my money.
3. I love to give money to those in need.
4. I use money to better my life and the lives of others.
5. I am the master of my money.
6. The money I give away always comes back to me multiplied.
7. I love using my money to improve the lives of others.
8. I use money to support good causes.
9. Money creates a positive impact on my life and the lives of others.
10. The more money I contribute, the more money I will make.
11. I am happy to pay my bills for all that they provide me.
12. I can use money to create a better life for myself and others.
13. I spend money on the things that matter to me most.
14. Having money enables me to grow as a person.
15. I use money to provide good things for myself and the people I love.
16. I spend money on things that will bring positive outcomes.
17. I am mindful of my wealth so it serves me and those around me.

18. I love having money because it allows me to do good things.
19. The more I give, the wealthier I become.
20. People benefit from my wealth and abundance.

Having More Than Enough Money

10 affirmations to attract more than enough money.

1. I always have more than enough money.
2. I am financially free.
3. Money is abundant to me.
4. I have more than enough money to fulfill my needs.
5. The universe provides enough money for everyone.
6. I have more money than I could ever spend.
7. I am a wealthy person and grateful for that.
8. I can easily afford whatever I want.
9. I am wealthy and happy.
10. I am worthy of the wealth I desire

You can shift from a negative mindset about money to one of abundance by repeating any of the above positive affirmations. When you consciously choose your thoughts, you are transforming your mindset and will become empowered to take control of your life. Money isn't going to manifest itself unless you truly believe it will and affirmations are a potent way to start confirming that you too are worthy of prosperity.

The Universe is infinite in its generosity and often, all we need to do is ask for something with open arms and let the Universe do its thing. What many of you may not realize is that we can aid that process along by taking certain actions and, in effect, *bend the Universe*. I am sure you are intrigued enough to find out more about that so let's move on to the last chapter.

For now, I hope that you begin to use affirmations in your everyday life as you cultivate the art of manifesting more money. Remember to stay positive, take action, and be grateful – you truly can achieve all of your dreams!

Key Points:

- *Affirmations are powerful positive statements that help us to focus on our goals.*
- *Affirmations change the way our subconscious shapes our identity.*
- *Follow the 7 golden rules for positive affirmations.*
- *The more frequently you use affirmations, the more success you will have.*
- *You can create your own or use ready-made affirmations.*
- *Different affirmations address different needs, depending on your desires.*
- *Affirmations can help you overcome your negative relationship with money.*

8

BENDING THE UNIVERSE – TAKING BACK CONTROL

"If you want to find the secrets of the universe, think in terms of energy, frequency, and vibrations." – Nikola Tesla

So far, we've talked a lot about the Universe and its infinite power of abundance. You will have heard many success stories about people who have used the law of attraction to send out positive messages to the Universe and have been rewarded with wealth, prosperity, and happiness. Celebrities like Oprah Winfrey, Jim Carrey, Will Smith, and Lady Gaga are well-known figures who put a large part of their success down to the law of attraction.

Many other people claim that it hasn't worked for them and they haven't achieved their goals. You might be one of them and wondering what else you can do. I've given you a lot of useful strategies to follow in this book, and in this last chapter, I'm going to reveal how you can successfully bring everything together so that you too can enjoy that abundance you have been reading about.

If you didn't get the job, the car, the house, the guy/girl, it's easy to become disheartened and feel that you are unlucky.

When you can't seem to earn more money and your expenses are outgrowing your income, it can feel as if the Universe has totally abandoned you. I can understand why you might see things that way, but the truth is that the Universe simply does what it does and responds to both positive and negative vibrations equally. It hasn't targetted you personally and said, "I'm going to make John's life a misery." Far from it; the Universe always responds to the frequencies you give out, whether positive or negative.

What is the Universe?

Wikipedia says that the universe is, "...all of space and time and their contents, including planets, stars, galaxies, and all other forms of matter and energy." There are many different kinds of energy, including kinetic, potential, elastic, chemical, radiant, and thermal, all of which we experience every second of every day without even noticing.

As Nikola Tesla rightly said, the universe can be understood if we think in terms of energy, frequency, and vibration. When you look at the atomic chart, every basic element consists of energy at different rates of vibration. Of course, we can't see it with the naked eye, but we know the phenomenon exists. These vibrations resonate on different frequencies and interact with the universe in a constant stream.

Even our minds are producing energy with our thoughts, transmitting each one out into the infinite superhighway of life. The law of attraction states that by changing your energetic vibration, you can change the way the universe responds to you. Positive energy vibrates at a higher frequency than negative energy so we receive what we think, for good or bad.

If you feel like the law of attraction isn't working for you, it may be because you have forgotten that the Universe abides by these simple laws of energy, frequency, and vibration. You are actually in control and in order to get what you want, you must resonate energy on the same frequency as what you have asked for. You can't resonate with negative energy and expect to receive anything positive – that's like trying to tune into your favorite radio station but setting the dial to the wrong number.

The fact is that you can take control of your life and 'bend the Universe' in your favor, once you understand how to do that. You don't need a Ph.D. in Quantum Physics or be born wealthy in order to qualify. All you need is to be open to new possibilities and more mindful of your thoughts and actions. Even if you don't create a vision board, do daily affirmations, or try manifesting your goals, you can still take some control over your life and attract positive energy from the Universe.

How we shape our reality

Our reality is shaped by invisible forces that we aren't aware of most of the time, and we often put things down to coincidence, luck, or destiny. These forces have an effect on how we live, what decisions we make, how we perceive our future, and what we manifest.

Our emotions

Often, it's our emotions that are controlling our behavior, and these are invisible forces that we can't see, but we know they are there because we feel them. Many of our successes and failures come down to the way we handle these emotions, with negative ones like anger and bitterness creating negative outcomes.

We are capable of experiencing a wide range of human emotions, from profound grief at the passing away of a loved one to unbridled joy at a birth, and everything in between. All of these feelings impact our actions and influence our lives in ways we aren't usually conscious of. If you are in a bad mood, you might be rude to someone; if you are in a good mood, you may be kind to another person. Whatever energy you give out to others creates a ripple effect that spreads out and the Universe is picking up on all of those vibes, whether you are aware of it or not.

Our decisions

Our emotions often affect the decisions we make, leading us to go one way or another, depending on how we feel. If you fail an important interview that could have brought you a promotion, you focus on your disappointment, which might lead you to lose self-confidence and not bother applying for a promotion again. Your action, or inaction, stems from how you are feeling about yourself, and, here again, you are sending out negative vibrations. If, on the other hand, you decide to improve, learn more, and upgrade your skills, this will enable you to stand a better chance of getting that promotion next time.

Our focus

It's really important to focus on the positives rather than the negatives and the more you do this, the more you will actually begin to manifest positive events in your life. When we constantly focus on our failures, we don't even see the opportunities for success, as if we develop blind spots. A good way to prove this is by doing a simple exercise:

Spend the next ten seconds looking around the room and count as many things as you can that are red.

Now that you have done that, how many blue items did you see?

Of course, you weren't focused on the color blue so probably didn't notice everything blue in the room. The red represents the things we choose to focus on in life, developing a kind of tunnel vision that prevents us from seeing anything else. Think of all the things you could have done today if you hadn't been so wrapped up in one particular idea or thought. The possibilities are truly endless.

Our questions

When we ask negative questions, we are going to receive negative answers – that's how the law of attraction works. If you ask yourself, "Why am I so unlucky?" you will continue to attract bad luck, unfortunately. This is because by asking such a negative question in the first place, you are sending a message to your brain that you deserve it, or that it's your fate, which will affect the way you approach everything.

You can easily turn that around by asking, "How can I attract what I want in life?" and your brain will start getting to work on how to achieve that. This isn't just about changing from negative to positive self-talk but has a much wider rippling effect. It allows you to leverage the power of the Universe to your advantage.

Try this experiment

I have a neat experiment for you to try and once you do it, you will truly see how you can manifest your goals by bending the Universe, in line with the law of attraction. I call this experiment 'Karmic Parking', although Karma is a concept that has several meanings, depending on who you talk to. Anyway, this is something that I've tried thousands of times and I've got to say: it works 100%.

When looking for a parking spot in your local city center or a busy mall, NEVER say to yourself that you won't find anywhere to park. Instead, ALWAYS say, "I will find a parking spot."

If you have a passenger in the car with you, tell them not to say things like, "The parking is a problem here", or "You'll never find anywhere to park today." In fact, they aren't to make any comments about parking at all. Gag them if you have to!

Do not discuss the difficulty of finding somewhere to park or let it slip into the conversation, and simply repeat to yourself that you will find a space.

You will find the perfect parking spot immediately.

I apply this strategy every time I drive into town and it really got me thinking that if I can control something as simple as finding a parking spot, what else can I control in my life? It may not seem like a big deal, but actually it is. I avoid getting stressed out in the morning, begin my workday in a much better mood, feel less flustered when I arrive at the office, and emit positive vibes all around. Try it and see for yourself!

Taking back control

When you think about making a cup of tea or coffee, your thought propels your body into action. Before you know it, you are enjoying a nice hot beverage and sending fuzzy feelings of pleasure back to your brain. Thought is so powerful that it can do that; it can control almost everything in your life, barring external events like the weather.

In the same way, we can utilize the power of the Universe to grant us our wishes but we need to create space for that reward to come back to us. Remember that the Universe abhors a vacuum so as soon as we create space by emitting positive energy, it will be filled with more of the same.

Holding on to negative memories, painful experiences, losses, and failures is cluttering up space in your life that could be filled with so many positive possibilities. You have to declutter your mind and your life, removing anything that is blocking you from moving on to pursue your goals. This requires time and effort, just as it would to sort out your wardrobes and cupboards at home, getting rid of anything you don't need anymore. When you create space for something new, you are saying to the Universe, "Here I am. I'm ready to receive your abundance."

Often, we dwell on disappointments and failure as something bad that has happened to us, instead of seeing how it can lead to another door opening. Experiencing a financial loss, for instance, can be a very jolting experience. We might go through a kind of grieving process and don't consider for a moment that what is happening can be a chance to enjoy a better future. We become stuck in a state of limbo, dwelling on our misfortune and unable to see beyond that.

Instead of spending your time and energy mourning over what has passed, allow yourself to be open to new possibilities and let the Universe do what it does best. Learn from the loss and look at what you would do differently next time. Surrender to what has happened and don't dwell on the negatives – it's done, past, and finished.

There is a simple equation you can follow if you really want to bend the universe in your favor. Basically, you need to give two things: your time and energy. If you want success, you need to spend time and energy. If you want to learn a new skill, you have to spend time and energy. If you want to be rich, you will need to spend time and energy.

You must be prepared to give something up (time and energy) to receive something greater. You might not get everything you desire right away, but think of it as accumulating credits with the Universe that you will be rewarded with at some point in the future.

Step out of your comfort zone

A lot of people feel trapped by their circumstances but don't do anything to change them because they tell themselves they have no other option. You always have other options, although they aren't easy to see when you are sitting in your comfort zone. Change is scary and taking risks can make you feel unsettled and nervous but by avoiding them, you are blocking your energy. When you are bold and daring, that positive message goes out to the Universe, telling it you are willing to grow, to be challenged, and to receive the rewards.

If you are afraid to take chances, you are already admitting you might fail, so you aren't likely to receive any positivity back in return. On the other hand, if you face your fears, you are creating more opportunities for growth and success. It doesn't have to be anything dramatic, and I'm not suggesting that you leave your day job without having secured another source of income first.

I deal with many clients on a daily basis who decided to go it alone, becoming entrepreneurs and business owners. The hardest part of the process for all of them was about making the right decision at the right time. With careful planning and great preparation, most of them were able to leave full-time jobs where they were underpaid and under-appreciated to go on to create a successful career for themselves. None of them have any regrets and never look back.

Think outside the box

The Universe is like a gigantic antenna, picking up any signals and amplifying them back. It's up to you to emit as many positive signals as possible if you want to enjoy the good things in life. One way to increase your chances is by thinking outside the box.

So you want to make more money? What are you doing to achieve that? If you are doing the same old thing, you aren't likely to get anywhere. You need to look for other ways to generate more money, which could be through passive income, side-hustles, or investments. There are lots of fantastic books out there on how to generate more income while still holding on to your day job, with **Millionaire Mind Crush** by Keith Everett being a great example.

Don't like where you are living but can't afford to upscale to a better area? What about house-flipping, where you buy a property at a low price and renovate it yourself? Don't have the skills to do that? How about taking an evening class on home renovation or watching YouTube videos on the subject – there are millions of them out there.

All of this activity will take you in the right direction, with your time and energy being used in a positive, productive way. Your signal will be received by the Universe – have no doubt about that.

Be enthusiastic about life

Life can be amazing and if you tune into positivity, it can only get better. Whatever it is that you want to achieve, enthusiasm goes a long way. It supercharges you to actively pursue your dreams and elevates your positive vibrations. Doing things half-heartedly or grudgingly only saps you of your energy, making any task seem ten times harder than it actually is. As a result, you will be less productive and more prone to give up before you have finished it.

If you can generate excitement each day, no matter what's on your agenda, you will send waves of positive vibes out to the Universe. Nobody likes a grump, and if you are acting like that, people will steer clear of you. In the same way, your negativity deflects anything good and only attracts negative energy back to you.

See the signs

The Universe is always sending out signs to you that you just don't see. You are probably so involved in trying to get by or leading your life that you aren't receptive to the signs, or don't understand them. It's likely that you aren't fully aware of the 'language' the Universe uses and can't always see the signs. Don't expect to see messages written in the sky or clouds in the shape of dollar bills, but do open up to an awareness of what is going on around you.

The Universe speaks through life itself and as conscious beings, we have the ability to learn from that once we understand how to decode it. Begin by asking questions and be prepared to receive answers, even if they are not the ones you were expecting. For example, if you are wondering how to make your first million, it could be that the answer demands you become more generous.

How will you know that? Because it has been looking you in the face every day – the homeless guy in the street, the stray dogs in your neighborhood, the local hospital in need of volunteers... it could be any number of things.

You can receive answers from the Universe through strangers, a random occurrence, or even while flicking through a magazine. It could be through a particular song you keep hearing or certain conversations about a specific topic that you pick up on over and over again. The Universe is boundless and always moving through your life, but you need to start looking and paying attention, instead of hoping things will just happen.

To become more aware of the signs the Universe puts out, you need to pay greater attention to yourself. Trust your gut instinct when you feel a certain way about a person or event and listen to what it is telling you. Do you have a good feeling about this person/situation/development or is there something not right about it? Our higher faculties are very in tune with the Universe, although we ignore them a lot of the time, replacing them with logic and reason.

This isn't always in our best interest though and when we overlook such signs, we could be missing out on great opportunities. You can improve your levels of awareness by practicing more meditation, mindfulness, or deep self-reflection, learning how to listen with greater clarity to your inner voice as it picks up signs from the Universe.

Be spontaneous

Having a daily or weekly routine is all well and good, but it can limit your chances of new experiences and exciting possibilities. We tend to get into routines because they make us feel comfortable, safe, and secure, which do serve a purpose although can hinder our potential for greater fulfillment.

Spontaneity is much more likely to connect you with the Universe through higher vibrations and bring you closer to achieving your goals. When a friend calls you and invites you to a party this Friday, don't turn them down simply because you always stay at home on Friday evenings and order Chinese. Be bold, daring, and adventurous – who knows what might happen if you do so?

Take a break from work even if it isn't officially break time, get out of the house when you are bored, drop the chores and go shopping, or book the first flight to somewhere fantastic. Whatever you do to break your routine will bring you valuable experience, perhaps chance encounters, new sensations, and more positive energy.

Pay it forward

I just loved the Warner Bros. movie called 'Pay It Forward' featuring Kevin Spacey and Helen Hunt when I first saw it back in 2000. The idea behind the title is that you do a favor for someone and tell them not to pay it back to you. Instead, they are to pay it forward to three other people who, in turn, each pay it forward to three more, and so on. This is the kind of action that the Universe responds to with even greater abundance and love and not only that, you are also creating a global wave of kindness. How cool is that!

I've seen how this works in real life and have witnessed the rewards of showing kindness, something that we are all capable of doing. It doesn't have to be a grand gesture or involve large amounts of money, but it does have to come from the heart without expecting anything in return. In the same way, when you receive the kindness of others, be prepared to pay that forward at the first chance you get and notice how good things begin to align up in your life. What could you do today to get the ball rolling?

The Universe always responds to your energy and by understanding more about how it works, you can gain greater happiness, joy, and prosperity.

When you raise your awareness, fine-tune your thoughts and follow the signs. It is always possible to lead your greatest life. Remember to stay open and express gratitude for everything you receive and most of all, stay positive!

Key Points:

- *The Universe responds to vibrational energy every second of our lives.*
- *We shape our reality through our emotions, focus, and questions.*

- *By taking control of our lives, we allow space for the Universe to flow through it.*
- *When you step out of your comfort zone, you are welcoming new possibilities.*
- *Thinking outside the box brings greater opportunities for success.*
- *Being enthusiastic generates a higher vibrational frequency.*
- *The Universe sends us signs that we can learn to interpret.*
- *Spontaneity is the secret to unlocking new experiences.*
- *When you pay kindness forward, it returns to you as abundance.*

CONCLUSION

We all love rags to riches stories and are familiar with fictional characters who went from humble beginnings to wealth and good fortune such as Cinderella, Oliver Twist, and Aladdin. Most of these stories have a moral to tell us about how being honest and kind will eventually pay off.

There are many real-life figures too, like Michael Schumacher, Sean Connery, and Rihanna, all of whom made their dreams come true in their chosen professions after starting life in relative poverty. The main message we get from these contemporary success stories is that talent and hard work go a long way. You may be born into a poor family or have a rough start in life, but you can succeed in the end.

Luck, talent, hard work, and persistence are all ways to achieve your life goals and when you embrace the law of attraction too, you are really tapping into infinite possibilities. No matter what your background is or what problems you have faced in life, it's never too late to turn that around and succeed. Many people struggle with money or have a problematic relationship with it, often feeling that they don't deserve to be rich or that they aren't good with money. I hope that I have dispelled some of those mind-myths and showed you that EVERYONE deserves wealth and prosperity.

Remember that the universe responds to the positive energy you put out and rewards you with positive results, while negative energy brings negative outcomes. Having a positive mindset is therefore key to getting what you want and it also leads to a happier, healthier, more fulfilled life.

The fundamental principle behind the law of attraction is that you will become what you think, making it possible for you to achieve your goals and materialize your dreams. After reading this book, you will have realized that there is a lot more to it than simply making a wish if you want the law of attraction to work for you.

We've talked about the many different strategies you should practice regularly in the above chapters, as well as some powerful tools to help you make more money. Once you begin to apply these, you will notice that abundance begins to manifest itself in numerous ways and as long as you remain positive, you will accumulate greater wealth in your life.

To recap, there are **7 crucial steps** that you must be willing to take in order to leverage the law of attraction to the full.

First of all, you must **decide** what it is that you want. Everyone would like to have more money, but how much do you want? Hundreds? Thousands? Millions? Are you aiming just to have enough to live a comfortable life or do you want to be a billionaire? It's extremely important to be clear about what you want if you wish to see results so don't be afraid to be specific when thinking about your goals.

Secondly, you have to **ask** the Universe to grant what you want by writing it down, visualizing it, and making affirmations that help you to manifest your desires. You must make a habit of asking for it daily, just as you would if you needed to train every day for a marathon that you plan to take part in. Practice makes perfect and as you do so, you are helping to reprogram your subconscious mind so it can tap into the energy stream of the Universe.

The third step involves **visualizing** what you want, which has been proven to be effective in helping us sharpen our skills to achieve our desires. When you practice visualization, your brain believes whatever you envision is real and creates new neural pathways that allow for greater drive and motivation. Vision boards can be extremely helpful in this process, but you need to make sure you also create bridging steps that will take you from where you are now to where you want to be in the future.

The next step on your path to successfully harnessing the law of attraction is to include **emotions** while manifesting your desires. You need to engage all of your senses when visualizing or making affirmations as that helps to create a mindset of believing you have already achieved your goals. We know that thoughts are energy and when we add positive emotions to those, they resonate on a much higher frequency because they are imbued with stronger feelings. The higher the vibration, the more likely the Universe is to respond.

You also need to express **gratitude** often, which is an extremely important element of the law of attraction. It's not all about receiving, but also about giving thanks for what you already have, which in turn raises your vibrations more. When you express gratitude for even the simplest things in your life, such as your family, good health, or food on the table, you will fully tune in to abundance rather than sending the negative vibrations of lack and scarcity.

The sixth step is one that many fail to do, and that is to take **action**. It is also the reason why a lot of people fail to achieve what they want because they haven't understood what the law of attraction is all about. It requires more than just wishing or thinking, but demands that you connect your reality with your dreams through actions. Your goals can be realized but you have to work hard, be consistent, and persevere if you want to reach a successful outcome.

Finally, you have to **trust** the process and believe wholeheartedly that the Universe will hear you and respond. It won't work if you give up after a few days or weeks, or fill your head with doubts and cynicism. All good things come with time and although you may not see immediate results, that doesn't mean the Universe isn't working in your favor. If you want to become a millionaire, you have to believe deep down that it is possible and remove any traces of doubt. Instead of self-sabotaging yourself, you need to be mindful of your thoughts and remain positive, no matter what.

In order to make your dreams come true, you might have to make sacrifices along the way and close some doors in order for others to open. You will face obstacles and challenges as you advance on your journey, which you should welcome as learning experiences. Trust that the Universe has put them there for a good reason and don't give up at the first hurdle. No one said it was going to be easy and as you come across stumbling blocks, view them as opportunities for growth and self-development. It's also necessary to create more space for abundance to flow in by decluttering your mind of negativity and self-doubt. You will need to stop holding on to old beliefs, self-limiting mindsets and habits that could prevent you from reaching your full potential.

Letting go of anything is never easy but as you welcome the law of attraction into your life, you will be rewarded with more joy and happiness than you ever thought possible. It will often require you to step out of your comfort zone and think outside the box, which will allow you to explore your limitations and become more aware of your thoughts and feelings. You can reshape your reality once you fully embrace the law of attraction, learn to read the signs the Universe is sending you, and live your life with optimism and enthusiasm.

I'll leave you with a powerful quote by Deepak Chopra, which I hope will resonate with you on every level and help bring you all the wealth you deserve:

"Truly wealthy people never worry about losing their money because they know that wherever money comes from there is an inexhaustible supply of it."

In other words, trust the Universe – it knows exactly what to do!

I hope that I have inspired you to think more about what you want to achieve in life, and hopefully will help you to achieve money and prosperity by using the law of attraction.

*If you enjoyed reading this book, please go to my **Amazon** page and leave an honest review!*

*You can also pick up my other two books on Amazon: **Love Yourself Deeply**, and **How To Make Friends Easily**.*

Please feel free to tell your friends and family about my work and share the love!

Thank you

Rebecca

www.ingramcontent.com/pod-product-compliance
Lightning Source LLC
Chambersburg PA
CBHW031545080526
44588CB00018B/2709